ALASKA'S
BROOKS RANGE

The Ultimate Mountains

John M. Kauffmann

The Mountaineers

Published by The Mountaineers
1011 SW Klickitat Way, Seattle, Washington 98134

Published simultaneously in Canada by Douglas & McIntyre, Ltd.,
1615 Venables Street, Vancouver, B.C. V5L 2H1

Published simultaneously in Great Britain by Cordee,
3a DeMontfort Street, Leicester, England, LE1 7HD

Manufactured in the United States of America

Edited by Sara Levant
Maps by Nick Gregoric
Cover design by Watson Graphics
Book design and typography by Choy-yee Kok
Cover photograph by Hulahula River region, Arctic National Wildlife Refuge, Alaska. © Art Wolfe

Permissions

The following publishers have generously granted permission to use extended quotations from copyrighted works: Excerpts from *Two in the Far North*, by Margaret E. Murie, are reprinted with permission of Alaska Northwest Books. Copyright (c) 1978 by Margaret E. Murie. * Excerpts from *Journey to the Far North*, by Olaus J. Murie, are reprinted courtesy Margaret E. Murie. * Excerpts from *Caribou and the Barrenlands*, by George Calef, are reprinted with permission of the Canadian Arctic Resource Committee. * The quotations from *Brooks Range Passage*, by David Cooper, are reprinted with permission of the publisher, The Mountaineers Books. * Collins, George L., "The Art and Politics of Park Planning and Preservation, 1920-1979," an oral history conducted 1978-1979 by Ann Lage, Regional Oral History Office, The Bancroft Library, University of California, Berkeley, 1980. Courtesy of The Bancroft Library. * Excerpts from *Midnight Wilderness*, by Debbie S. Miller, are reprinted with permission of Sierra Club Books. * Excerpts from *Koviashuvik*, by Sam Wright, are reprinted with permission of Sierra Club Books. * The excerpt from *Make Prayers to the Raven*, by Richard K. Nelson, is reprinted with permission of the University of Chicago Press. Copyright (c) 1983 by the University of Chicago Press. * Excerpts from *Ten Thousand Miles with a Dog Sled*, by Hudson Stuck, are courtesy of Charles Scribner's Sons. *(Page 192 constitutes a continuation of the copyright page.)*

Library of Congress Cataloging in Publication Data

Kauffmann, John M.
    Alaska's Brooks Range: the ultimate mountains/John M. Kauffmann.
      p. cm.
    Includes bibliographical references and index.
    ISBN 0-89886-346-5. –ISBN 0-89886-347-3 (pbk.)
    1. Brooks Range (Alaska)—History. 2. Brooks Range (Alaska)—Geography. 3. Natural history—Alaska—Brooks Range. I. Title.
F912.B75K38 1992
979.8'7–dc20
92-25945
CIP

Printed on acid-free paper

During my years of Alaskan residence, my home in Anchorage on Kershner Avenue became a happy rendezvous and rallying place for many colleagues and other friends living in Alaska or arriving there to help in the cause of protecting its wild magnificence. Students, government officials, environmental leaders, old friends and young acquaintances who themselves became firm friends very soon, all contributed conviviality exceeded only by dedication. Some began to call us The Kershner Club. Mardy Murie was a specially honored member, Ted Swem, another. The roster is long, often distinguished, always characterized by warm hearts, vim, and faith.

To Mardy, Ted, and all the other members of The Kershner Club this book is thankfully and affectionately dedicated.

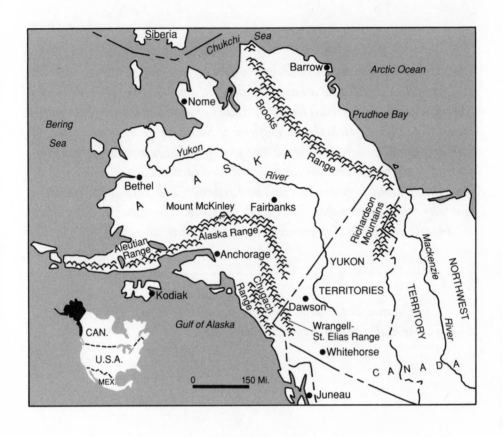

Siberia

Chukchi Sea

Brooks Range

Barrow

Arctic Ocean

Nome

Prudhoe Bay

Bering Sea

Yukon River

A L A S K A

Bethel

Mount McKinley

Fairbanks

Richardson Mountains

Aleutian Range

Alaska Range

Anchorage

YUKON

Mackenzie River

NORTHWEST

Kodiak

Chugach Range

TERRITORIES

Dawson

TERRITORY

CAN.

Gulf of Alaska

Wrangell-
St. Elias Range

U.S.A.

Whitehorse

C A N A D A

MEX.

0   150 Mi.

Juneau

4

CONTENTS

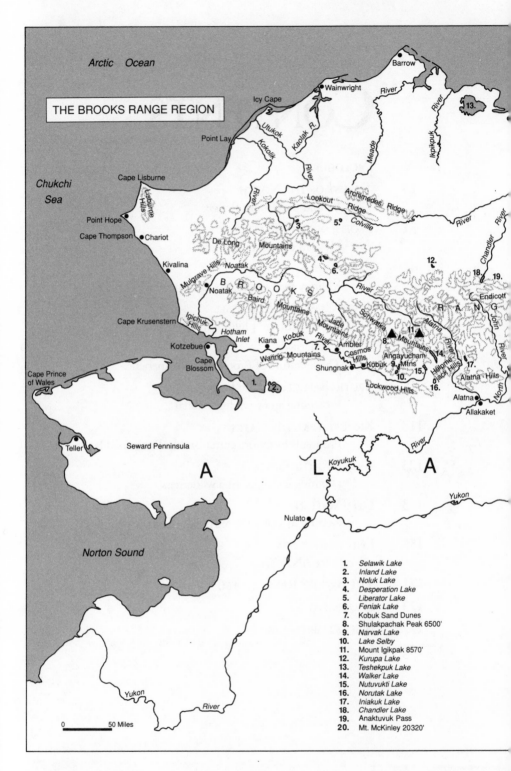

THE BROOKS RANGE REGION

Arctic Ocean

Chukchi Sea

Barrow
Wainwright
Icy Cape
Point Lay
Cape Lisburne
Point Hope
Cape Thompson Chariot
Kivalina
Cape Krusenstern
Kotzebue
Cape Prince of Wales
Teller
Seward Penninsula
Norton Sound

Lisburne Hills
Mulgrave Hills
De Long Mountains
Noatak
Noatak
Baird
BROOKS Mountains
Igichuk Hills
Hotham Inlet
Cape Blossom
Kiana
Waring Mountains
Jade Mountains
Kobuk River
Shungnak
Ambler
Cosmos Hills
Kobuk
Angayucham Mtns
Lookwood Hills

Lookout Ridge
Archimedes Ridge
Colville
Meade River
Kaolak R.
Utukok
Kokolik
River
Ikpikpuk River

Schwatka Mountains
Alatna River
Alatna Hills
Endicott
RANGE
John River
Haiome Black Hills
Alatna
Allakaket
Chandler River
North

Koyukuk
ALA
Yukon
Nulato
Yukon
River

1. Selawik Lake
2. Inland Lake
3. Noluk Lake
4. Desperation Lake
5. Liberator Lake
6. Feniak Lake
7. Kobuk Sand Dunes
8. Shulakpachak Peak 6500'
9. Narvak Lake
10. Lake Selby
11. Mount Igikpak 8570'
12. Kurupa Lake
13. Teshekpuk Lake
14. Walker Lake
15. Nutuvukti Lake
16. Norutak Lake
17. Iniakuk Lake
18. Chandler Lake
19. Anaktuvuk Pass
20. Mt. McKinley 20320'

0   50 Miles

6

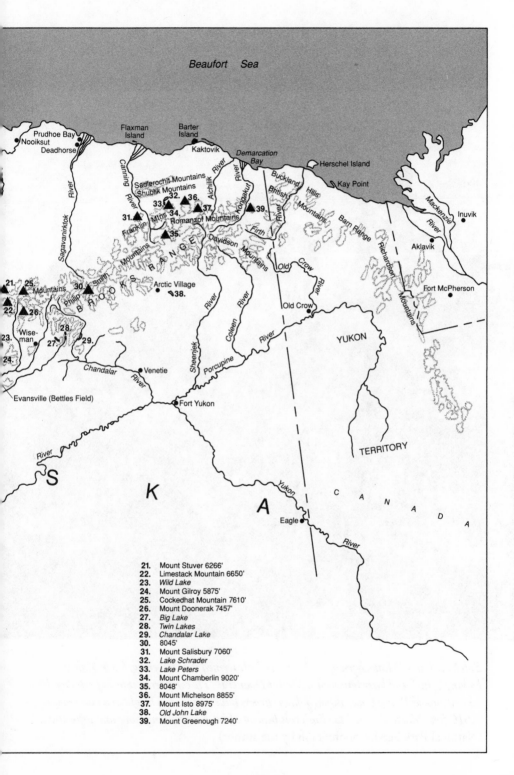

Beaufort   Sea

Prudhoe Bay
Nooiksut
Deadhorse
Flaxman Island
Barter Island
Kaktovik
Demarcation Bay
Herschel Island
Kay Point
Inuvik
Aklavik
Fort McPherson
Sadlerochit Mountains
Shublik Mountains
Canning River
Aichilik River
Kongakut River
Buckland Hills
British Mountains
Barn Range
Mackenzie River
Richardson Mountains
Sagavanirktok River
Franklin Mountains
Romanzof Mountains
Davidson Mountains
Firth River
Old Crow River
Smith Mountains
Arctic Village
Philip
BROOKS RANGE
Sheenjek River
Coleen River
Porcupine River
Old Crow
YUKON
Wise-man
Chandalar
Venetie
Evansville (Bettles Field)
Fort Yukon
River
S
K
A
Yukon
TERRITORY
C A N A D A
Eagle
River

21. Mount Stuver 6266'
22. Limestack Mountain 6650'
23. *Wild Lake*
24. Mount Gilroy 5875'
25. Cockedhat Mountain 7610'
26. Mount Doonerak 7457'
27. *Big Lake*
28. *Twin Lakes*
29. *Chandalar Lake*
30. 8045'
31. Mount Salisbury 7060'
32. *Lake Schrader*
33. *Lake Peters*
34. Mount Chamberlin 9020'
35. 8048'
36. Mount Michelson 8855'
37. Mount Isto 8975'
38. *Old John Lake*
39. Mount Greenough 7240'

Bob Marshall's "Matterhorn of the Koyukuk." He termed it a "towering, black, unscalable-looking giant" and later renamed it Mount Doonerak. He considered it to be probably the highest Brooks Range peak, although later surveys have recorded its height at a more modest 7,610 feet. Marshall tried to climb this beacon of his Brooks Range love and aspiration. (National Park Service photograph by the author)

PROLOGUE

This windswept country is so revealing that you see what you are spiritually, morally.
—Benjamin Wyer Bragonier

The gaunt peaks of the Brooks Range are North America's ultimate mountains. Beyond their far slope, the continent slips beneath the ice of arctic seas. A few ranges and parts of ranges stand even closer to the pole—in Siberia, on Ellesmere Island—but none so extensive or important. The Brooks is the northernmost major mountain range in the world, stretching from Canada's Yukon Territory across the entire breadth of Alaska as a rampart more than seven hundred miles long.

A web of life covers it so tenuously as to prompt wonder that it can survive, let alone thrive, in that grim climate. Under a wan but almost perpetual summer sun, life communities are simple but delicately attuned, and some species are stretched to their limit. Others glory in their arctic element, some of them arriving from afar to nest and feed. Here are displayed most of the last great wildlife spectacles in North America. The largest remaining herds of caribou filter by the hundreds of thousands through the Brooks Range twice each year—north to calve, south for winter forage and shelter. Peregrines and gyrfalcons still command arctic eyries. Wolf packs lope the tundra, whereon imperial grizzlies also stride.

These all indicate that this mountain country, standing on the ragged edge of humanity's influence, is as yet nearly pristine. Glittering in the arctic night of winter, or aglow with the long low rays of summer's midnight sun, this range is clearly one of the few remaining regions of Earth that is only beginning to show a faint tarnish of degradation. And so it is an ultimate range in terms of human experience and opportunity as well: a last great mountain wilderness, a last frontier—not to exploit but to keep as it has always been.

Not so long ago, the American frontier lay along the crest of the Appalachian Range; later, the Rockies; then, finally, north to where human enterprise dug amid the formidable ranges of Alaska. With the discovery and development of arctic oil,

9

even the Brooks Range has been enveloped and breached. The mountains themselves remain largely a fastness, however, even though well mapped and probed, and
increasingly visited. Now they form a vast wild reserve, protected in four giant units
of the National Park System, in a huge national wildlife refuge and two coastal refuge
units. Most of the land is formally dedicated wilderness, the largest such region in
the world. There people who are hunter-gatherers can still pursue their age-old way
of life.

With no more land frontier that people can experience, the United States
has set aside this last wild mountain expanse so that future generations may always

Newborn caribou calf. (U.S. Fish and Wildlife Service photograph by Wilbur Mills)

have a place to comprehend what New World means, may feel the pulse of ancient wildlife cycles and taste what tempered the character of their forebears. Canada has joined in the protection. This yet remains a country to be taken on its own stern but exhilarating terms. It is a place where one can wonder, respectful of subtleties of nature as crushable as a flower. It is a place to study and learn how best to fit in without destroying the scheme of life so exquisitely evolved on this planet. Existence in pristine country has become a rare experience in most of the world. Protected, the Brooks Range can perpetuate a sense of what discovery and solitude can mean to the human spirit.

THRUST
OF
THE NORTH

Perhaps the most beautiful place in all the world.

—Jimmy Carter

First of all, there is the light. In the long winter, dawn soon becomes gloaming, fading into a darkness shimmered with auroras or lashed dimly white with snow. But in summer! In summer a sun returned pours glowing magic upon all times and situations. Darkness is banished, and perpetual light suffuses the land.

The long low rays sculpt and gild, so that each ridge, each rock and scarp stands brilliant in its own dimensionality. The smallest plant turns vibrant and luminous. Even as clouds enwrap the summits and mists come down, the light's enchantment can make a nimbus of the storm as rainbows arch. The frozen foundations of this world, so stern and unforgiving, are, for a time, forgotten under a kind, caressing spell. They are there, nevertheless, grimly close beneath the flowers, waiting for the delicate light so soon to weaken and to die. Then shall arctic reality return.

There is silence, the great natural silence, aura of many mutterings, rustlings, and aerie songs. A rock falls. Waters murmur, lap, and plash. Wind soughs across a sea of tiny leaves. A wolf may howl, a ground squirrel chirp. Raven and falcon croak and cry, and ptarmigan cluck amid the willows. The rumble of thunder may echo the softer thunder of ten thousand rumbling caribou.

But such sounds are merely orchestrations of a wild Quiet, a quiet Wild. It commands respectful, careful listening, just as the light commands a respectful, grateful gaze.

Contorted rock layers thrust upward as if to buttress Cockedhat Mountain in the central Brooks Range. (National Park Service photograph by the author)

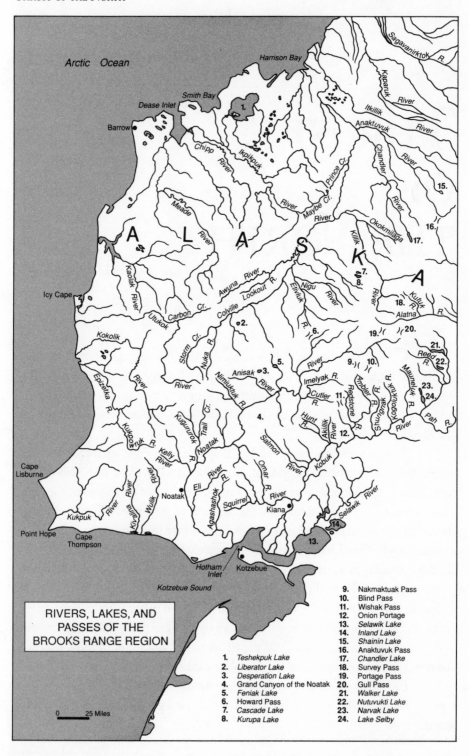

RIVERS, LAKES, AND
PASSES OF THE
BROOKS RANGE REGION

0   25 Miles

1. Teshekpuk Lake
2. Liberator Lake
3. Desperation Lake
4. Grand Canyon of the Noatak
5. Feniak Lake
6. Howard Pass
7. Cascade Lake
8. Kurupa Lake
9. Nakmaktuak Pass
10. Blind Pass
11. Wishak Pass
12. Onion Portage
13. Selawik Lake
14. Inland Lake
15. Shainin Lake
16. Anaktuvuk Pass
17. Chandler Lake
18. Survey Pass
19. Portage Pass
20. Gull Pass
21. Walker Lake
22. Nutuvukti Lake
23. Narvak Lake
24. Lake Selby

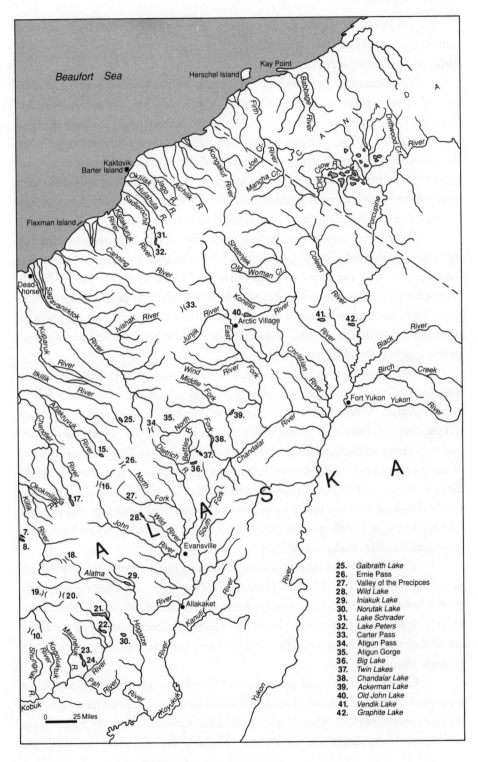

Beaufort Sea

Kay Point
Herschel Island
Kaktovik
Barter Island
Oktilak
Flaxman Island
Dead horse

25. Galbraith Lake
26. Ernie Pass
27. Valley of the Precipces
28. Wild Lake
29. Iniakuk Lake
30. Norutak Lake
31. Lake Schrader
32. Lake Peters
33. Carter Pass
34. Atigun Pass
35. Atigun Gorge
36. Big Lake
37. Twin Lakes
38. Chandalar Lake
39. Ackerman Lake
40. Old John Lake
41. Vendik Lake
42. Graphite Lake

0   25 Miles

15

And there are the rocks, the horde of serried peaks. Ordered only by their valleys, they stand half-naked, confused, still reeling, it would seem, from the vast forces of their geologic past.

As blocks of sea ice crunch up into pressure ridges, so was this Brooks Range formed. That is what the Native people of arctic Alaska have always maintained. Geologists agree, although noting that the process spanned many millions of years. A current author on such geologic processes once offered me a similar analogy: "Your Brooks Range is a pile of driftwood," said John McPhee. His comment reflects what most scientists now surmise: that Alaska itself is a conglomeration of drifted bits and pieces of the Earth cemented together into the huge right fist of North America that its citizens, ancient and modern, have called The Great Land.

As for the Brooks—the ultimate mountains, the last, the northernmost of the ranges now heaved glistening across North America's vast landscapes—these may have been the first, the very first sticks in the pile. Once they were part of North America's spine, geologists infer. They were built of sands and mud probably washed down from eastern lands, and of the calcium carbonate formed from the shells of myriad creatures that lived and died in shallow seas. Now they have been transfigured by the ages into Brooks Range crags.

Inexorably inching, another of Earth's great crustal plates rammed into this western continental edge, perhaps bearing a flotilla of volcanic islands or a slab of oceanic plateau. When the two plates closed and crushed together, the oceanic crust did the unusual. Instead of diving under the continental mass, it rode up onto it, peeling formations back upon themselves, slivering them, mashing and fusing many of the rocks into new consistencies. Entire geologic sequences were turned upside down or thrust over one another—cut and shuffled like a deck of cards. Then the whole chunk of territory broke loose from its continental moorings and pivoted counterclockwise, bending westward to rest at a right angle to the Rocky Mountain chain and become Alaska's northland.

The collision depressed the crust for a time, but it rebounded, perhaps to near-Himalayan heights. Deep, old intrusions of molten rock welled up and, with overlying rock masses now worn away, the exposed granites now form some of the range's biggest and most striking bastions. However, other, even higher summits are of a different, a metamorphic, rock that was squeezed in some stupendous geologic vise.

Geologists have made progress in sorting things out, picking through the topsy-turvy jumble for familiar and unfamiliar formations. They have recorded the rare serpentines and other deep-earth igneous masses. They have matched up and mapped the sandstone, schist, and conglomerate, the shale and slate, the

16

limestone and the marble, tracing some formations for hundreds of miles. Assemblages of rock beneath the Arctic Coast reoccur in far, high mountains, often contrasting sharply with adjacent formations there. But all along this land, stirred and beaten as by a giant's spoon, geologist after geologist uses the same term for the havoc: "mind-boggling."

Plate tectonics crunched up this vast flotsam, and ice ages, at least four of them, succeeded as sculptors of the agglomerated rock. Marks of the most recent of these are still fresh upon the land. Although there were local ice advances as recently as four or five thousand years ago, the region is no longer the active glacial area one finds at Denali, the Wrangell Mountains, or Glacier Bay. In the north, paradoxically, the big ice is nearly all gone, and only a hundred or so small residual glaciers remain pocketed among the higher peaks. A long-term change of weather has cut off the heavy snows of yesteryear.

In the primer of the Arctic, one basic understanding comes first: Ice has shaped everything. Steven B. Young presents the lesson best in *To the Arctic*:

> *It has sculpted the landforms through ancient glaciers. It has shattered the rocks, heaved the soil, and dammed the rivers. It has the final say on whether any organism will live or die. Perhaps most important, it provides a challenge to every living thing to adapt, to change, to improvise, and to survive. Nothing in the polar regions escapes the ice.*

In the Brooks Range, the sculpture wrought by the departed ice is spectacular, and there is no temperate climate like New England's to gentle and soften the landscape and cloak the nudity of the land. In the Brooks, the ice has drawn back only to bare its handiwork of broad U-shaped canyons, hanging valleys, gouged-out cirques and tarns, and morainal lakes. All the classic glacial morphology is there to see, with just enough healing of the rawness to give it grace without masking form and the awesome evidence of process. The Brooks Range is gauntly beautiful. Limestones forming parts of its core have been carved by ice and dissolved by water into fantastic crags and canyons. They are largely bare, for alpine plants prefer a more acidic environment. Bare also are the dream-world monoliths that tower wherever granite has intruded.

Across other glacier-gnawed ribs of rock is drawn a skin of vegetation so thin and slow-growing that the average temperate-zone human being has difficulty realizing how tenuous it is.

The southern flanks of the Brooks Range are cloaked by the boreal forest: sparse stands of white and black spruce, paper birch, aspen, and "cottonwood" (balsam poplar) that are locally used but too poor to be of much commercial interest. The Russians called this *taiga*, a land of sparse, dwarfed conifers, and the word has passed into English usage.

Among the taiga trees, so slender, so scattered, stretch the carpets of mixed sedges, grasses, heaths, and shrubby trees that will continue leagues northward as tundra. Thickets of willow and alder crowd along stream courses and cloak wet hillsides. On uplands, the ground may be golden with expanses of caribou lichen or glinting with the shiny leaflets of dwarf birch. Willow patches flash white as wind turns upward the pale undersurfaces of their leaves. On banks and hills, magenta expanses of fireweed heal the scars of the lightning fires that periodically rage across the land and set off fresh cycles of plant succession.

There are slopes, too, where the trees tilt crazily—the result of solufluction, the sliding of the thawed topsoil in which they are rooted over the frozen ground beneath. This is the land of permafrost, which is sometimes thousands of feet in depth. Such ground ice can crack land surfaces into odd geometric patterns, or squeeze up pingos—ice-filled pimples of old lake bottom or gravel, some more than a hundred feet high. With only the thin mantle of tundra to insulate it, the frozen ground slumps and melts into ever-widening sloughs and ponds if that sod is stripped away.

Although once heavy with glaciers, and despite what seems to be an endless procession of rains and snows, the Brooks Range receives less, and in many places much less, than twenty inches of precipitation per year. In places with as little as five inches, the Arctic Slope would be a virtual desert were it not for the coolness that inhibits evaporation and the frost that seals off downward seepage. These factors keep the tundra a soggy sponge.

A thin and scattered boreal forest straggles northward across the range until a last spruce stands alone. Although poplars weather the north even farther, the conifers stop short of the Arctic Divide, a notable exception being in the Firth River Valley in the eastern Brooks. There the southern weather penetrates far north, as at the Mackenzie River Delta, where a spruce forest extends almost to the Arctic Ocean. Forester Robert Marshall believed that the slow-growing spruces of the central Brooks Range simply had not had time to seed northward. He made several seed plantings to induce an extension of the tree line, but they were unsuccessful, perhaps because of ill-adapted seed brought from elsewhere.

Passing the last trees is a poignant experience, especially to people used to them. The last spruce along the North Slope haul road (the Dalton Highway) was marked by a special sign. And to human beings whose hunter forebears watched for food from forest shelter, a return to trees brings a special gladness—like seeing old friends. Float down the Noatak River for two weeks through tundra, passing only some patches of shrubby willows or a rare small grove or two of poplars, and the first scrawny sentinels of the boreal forest seem beautiful indeed. Climb around the canyon at Nakmaktuak Pass, trudge over the last horizon and behold, a thousand feet below, the Ambler Valley full of forest. There at last is shelter.

Northwest Passage navigator Roald Amundsen, who traveled southward up the Firth Valley in 1905, told how excited he grew as he neared the tree line: "When at length the first fir [spruce] tree stood out against the sky up on the ridge—a very diminutive, battered little Christmas tree, hanging out of a crevice—it produced a wonderful sensation, reminding me that we were now out of Polar regions and on more homely human ground."

Forest depth may be welcome, but with it breadth disappears. Gone are the sweeping winds and wide dimensions. In contrast to forest thickets, shadows, lurkings, the tundra is a country of freedom—freedom to view and observe. Exhilaration comes in breaking out of density into openness. Those dawn-of-humanity hunters must have felt it as they left forest hiding places in pursuit of grassland game.

From the air—from any great distance—the tundra can look like a lawn. Not so. Its most notorious form is tussock tundra, patchy in the mountains but sweeping across their northern slopes in a tussock tide. Like the moors of Scotland, but on a far vaster scale, tussock tundra spreads an ominous apron below the peaks and ridges of the range.

Tussocks are formed by the *Eriphora*, the sedges known as cottongrass or Alaskan cotton, which blow their fluffy white seeds across the land. They and associated plants grow into mushroom-shaped mounds a foot or more high with basketball-size tops, and traversing them is like running an obstacle course. They tip when stepped upon, and there is often bog between them. Someone has estimated that there are five trillion tussocks in arctic Alaska alone. Knowing them and seeing them in their oceanic expanse makes the heart quail, for early exhaustion awaits the person doomed to cross much tussock tundra.

Tussocks or no, tundra is hummocky, its low-growing or prostrate heaths and dwarf trees masking the underlying truth of rocks and holes that test unwary ankles. Nevertheless, some people have mastered the hiking of it with a dancer's instincts. Keith Nyitray, who made an eight-month-long traverse of the entire

Brooks Range in 1989–1990, accompanied only by his part-wolf companion Smoke, crossed tundra easily with what he calls the "tundra two-step." During the summertime, he wore sneakers for his danced hiking.

For the less coordinated, however, tundra is not to be crossed with an easy or measured pace, let alone striding. They will find themselves staggering across it gracelessly in what can be best described as a controlled stumble. As Lois Crisler pointed out in *Arctic Wild*, "On tundra one cannot get into a rhythm or swing, or take even two steps together without looking." Only on the high fells, where just a skim of vegetation covers firm, stony ground, can one swing one's legs and plant one's feet with reasonable confidence, free to raise one's eyes to enjoy the exhilarating scene.

There is endless, intricate beauty to be viewed even with eyes fixed upon the ground, however. Tundra patterns of vegetation are exquisite, with an elfin delicacy. It is like crewelwork or embroidery, done with living roots and stems, leaves and flowers, pods and berries. The patterns, dictated by moisture, exposure, disturbance, and nutrients, become predictable, at least in general terms, and it is lovely repetition. Component species are few compared with the plant communities of warmer climates, but their soon familiar designs intertwine endlessly in delicate elegance. Ecologist David J. Cooper, author of *Brooks Range Passage,* has written, "The whole composition of various dwarf forms and brilliant colors makes this three-inch-high layer of vegetation the most amazing entity anyone could ever hope to see."

Cooper also mentions the textural qualities of tundra, its tactile beauty: "I run my hands through the vegetation at my side. The cottongrass is stiff though flexible, the birch is brittle, other plants are smooth and soft. The lichens and mosses are wet, hairy, silky, and spongy." There are also the subtlest of perfumes, as well as the astringent fragrance of Labrador tea. A blind person can understand and enjoy the tundra.

Much has been written about the fragility of tundra, its tearing so slow to heal. Actually, its plants are among the toughest on Earth, designed to withstand some of the most rigorous living conditions imaginable. Tundra life means bitter cold, gales that abrade and desiccate, smothering snow, slipping earth, a short, almost perpetual flood of light, and then long months of darkness.

In the lichens, a partnership of fungus and alga has been formed in order to survive where no green-leafed plant could endure. Lichens produce food in any temperature above freezing, using moisture directly, without the need of the vascular system that higher forms of plant life must build. Robert Marshall noted that lichens are estimated to cover a quarter of the vegetated surface of Alaska. They are vegetational pioneers, slowly, subtly, constantly helping to turn rock into soil.

The mosses also ask little and make the most of minimal water and warmth, curling tightly against adversity. Among the strategies of vascular plants are cushion shapes that foil the wind and catch the light, or growth in rosettes that are snugly close to the warmer air at soil's surface. Tundra plants are likely to be symmetrical, for sources of nourishment may come from any direction. They are likely also to lie flat in mats beneath the wind and to have creeping root systems that replace old ones torn away by animals or weather.

Hardy grasses and sedges have the advantages of narrow, wind-resistant leaves and stems, and small, efficient flowers. The evergreen heaths, with lower photosynthesis and respiration rates, can get along on less than the leaf-shedding plants. The old leaves of the heaths as well as the new are productive and can store food reserves that need not be used for a complete releafing every season.

For some tundra plants, succulence is a reserve against desiccation. Hairiness of leaf also insulates against water loss from high winds, diffuses strong light, and traps heat. Many tundra plants are generously endowed with red anthocyanin pigments that can convert the incident light of cold early spring into heat needed to warm plant tissues. The flower of the mountain avens operates like a sunflower turning to catch the sun.

The tundra has few annuals. They require too much energy to flower and produce seed in a single year. Indeed, some of the flowering perennials take more than one season—and some take years—to complete one seed-ripening cycle. A flower bud started the previous year and protected underground is quicker to flower and receive the high summer warmth necessary to get the heat required for ripening. Some tundra plants are ten or fifteen years old before they flower. Many plants reproduce vegetatively from runners, underground sprouting stems, or bulbs. They need not expend the energy to flower and ripen seeds at all in order to reproduce, and can draw on the reserves of parent plants.

When tundra plants do flower, they bloom in an astounding burst of prodigal energy, drawing down their reserves until the full heat of summer can ripen their seeds. They use the last rays of the season to rebuild tissues.

Although summer's light shines constantly for a month on the south side of the range and for more than two on the north, it is wan—oblique from a southern sun. Yet summer is so long overshadowed by arctic winter that, when life riots forth, it is with a vigor that astonishes anyone who walks the tundra in its flowering time. Emerging from nine wintry months, the tundra jewels itself in countless suites, as each of the limited number of plant species responds to light and warmth and unlocked moisture from its special vantage place. Snow, the presence and depth of which so rules tundra plants, is a major manager of the flowering. As the snowy curtain draws back, the show begins. If snow lingers, it waters the plants as it releases them from its protective blanketing against a deadly wind.

It all goes so quickly, this hail-and-farewell of tundra blooming! On arctic walks in summer, every stage, from bud to flower, through seed and reddening autumnal leaf, can often be seen simultaneously. There is so little time. And while the temperate world basks in the long golden radiance of late summer, the tundra blazes with autumn foliage. It is already an oriental carpet of scarlet, orange, gold, and bronze, its tiny plants making an elfin version of New England's early October.

Despite all this vigor, this annual burst of living glory, the Arctic is a very unproductive land. It is slow to grow, slow to heal, and that is the truth behind its oft-mentioned fragility. "The beat of the tundra is slow indeed," write Ann Zwinger and Beatrice Willard in *Land Above the Trees,* pointing out that its production is about three percent of that of a good lowland meadow. They call the cushions of moss fast-growing for tundra plants: half an inch in five years. Lois Crisler measured lichens at a sixteenth of an inch of annual growth that may need up to forty years to recuperate from the munching and tread of a passing caribou herd. Biologist Olaus Murie found a white spruce ten inches in diameter and almost 300 years old. Robert Marshall told of a black spruce three inches in diameter and 346 years old, and reported trees requiring thirty to thirty-five years to attain four and a half feet. Botanist John Dennis of the National Park Service found spruce seedlings twenty-five years old and a foot tall. They were at a campsite where someone had pulled up sphagnum moss for a bed. He estimated that ten years would be required for that moss to regenerate.

The life of the tundra, plant and animal, is adapted to survive there. Human beings, physiologically, are not. Yet it is man, ironically, whose slightest action can wipe out tundra life for generations. Impacts seem to last forever in this hemophiliac land that bleeds endlessly when it is cut and its underlying permafrost allowed to thaw. Wounds gape and deepen. In a region where soil formation proceeds at a fraction of an inch in a century, chemical breakdown is slow. Scientists have detected the effects of human wastes from Inupiat settlements centuries after the inhabitants have gone. Zwinger and Willard have emphasized that there is no natural destruction of the tundra that compares to man's. Recovery from ten days of concentrated trampling can take up to a thousand times longer than in more opulent ecosystems. Even the pressure of a snow machine on the snow produces a compacting that can long alter the regime beneath for plant and animal alike.

Most of us are temperate zone beings, and we simply cannot conceive of such low productivity and easily disrupted dependencies. In our experience, nature heals quickly if we exercise reasonable care. Last year's campsite is soon overgrown as vegetation again takes over. In old fields, trees spring up like weeds. It is virtually

Caribou lichen and other tundra vegetation. (National Park Service photograph)

impossible to fish out a good warm-water pond well stocked with bass and bluegills. Most of today's Alaskans were once accustomed to warmer, more flourishing climes. Even in Anchorage, the kids racing around on snow machines, knocking over young trees as they might do to scrub pines "back home" in Virginia, do not realize that those Alaskan trees may be eight times as old as they are. And they probably don't care. They have not been educated to care.

At first gaze, the Brooks Range appears to be a mineral and vegetable domain. Like the surface of a stormy sea, the region seems devoid of animality. At length, however, that reveals itself in a flutter, a buzz, a scurrying under the rocks.

Much of it has the same delicacy and elegance as the vegetation; some matches the topographic majesty. But animal life in the north is meager. Except at times and places of breeding and migration, one does not get an eyeful promptly. Perhaps it is wildlife photographs that have raised our hopes of seeing a sheep on every crag, the valleys thronged with caribou as wolf and bear rove the mountainsides. Because of photography, one half expects in the Arctic to see African fecundity or displays of a bygone Great Plains ecology, with bison and antelope herds a million strong. Compared to these imaginings, the Brooks Range wilds do seem empty.

The spectacle exists, however, from vole to bear. Again, it is a matter of low productivity, of life stretched across vast spaces, but exquisitely adapted to survive. It takes a hundred square miles to support a grizzly bear in the north, they say; almost as much for a wolf. Caribou must travel constantly, else they will overbrowse their range.

Animal life in the Brooks Range has a presence all out of proportion to its actual density. One follows its trails through the willows, wondering how many moose it took to beat such a path. Caribou and sheep trails lace the ridges, the slopes of talus and scree, with patterns so clearly worn that one is reminded of cattle paths across Appalachian pastures. But how many hooves, how many centuries has it taken to pulverize those rocks into a graveled trail?

On a narrow canyon rim, I have been awed by broad depressions paced into the hard ground. This was where the bears have walked, year after year, generation to generation, placing their great paws in their predecessors' tread. There are fresh signs as well: the huge hole torn in the tundra to dig out a ground squirrel, and that pile of excrement that says "Bear!" "How fresh, how fresh?" is the ever-apprehensive question.

The noblest signatures, written in John Hancock boldness across a sandbar while humans sleep nearby, are made by the saucer-sized paws of wolves. Not worrisome, these, but so essentially symbolic of the wilds that one catches breath in seeing them. Here is the music of the wilderness written out, note by printed note, on a stave of strand. Hear it sung of an evening, and the sound somehow transmutes to boreal light. The doomsday tread of dinosaur in rock is awesome indeed. The carved incantations of a bygone race bespeak an ancient lore. But these glyphs were made last night! The wolf is present in the Brooks, a part of its soul. It is not necessary to see the animal in order to understand the significance of that.

But Brooks Range wildlife is certainly not known only through signs and symbols. It seems to bloom with the plants. The sunlit tundra is abrim with insects. One walks through birdsong. Ptarmigan, turning brown after winter's white plumage, flush from the willows. Nesting migrants are everywhere—more than a hundred species—newly arrived from Siberia, from Mexico, from Chesapeake Bay, from Antarctica. Snow buntings, whitest of songbirds, have flurried in behind retreating snows. Asian bluethroats, uncommon even in Alaska, are found nowhere else in the United States. Golden plovers have arrived from the pampas and join least sandpipers daintily searching at water's edge. Phalaropes pertly ride a pond's rippling. A jaeger hovers in lethal elegance. With deep wing beats, tattlers swoop and bank like swallows, singing their long, lovely song. Evenings bring the liquid notes of the gray-cheeked thrush. Lapland longspurs pour forth melody in every weather.

Peer closely at the tundra, and the scurrying of a vole will indicate a whole society that lives under the sedges, in the rocks, under the snow. The little arctic ground squirrel will scold from his burrow mouth, and in this scaleless world, a fat furry marmot may, at a distance, appear to be a bear. Far more populous than the caribou, and at least as important in arctic life, small mammals are key links in the food chain. They take the energy that sunlight brings to plants and convert it into a form—themselves—upon which all of the predators largely subsist. Many have secrets tantalizing to science: How do ground squirrels, one of the few true hibernators, find a bed amid the permafrost and regulate their bodies to outlast winter? How do tiny shrews, with their incredibly high metabolism, manage to survive at all when their insect food is gone?

Despite the subtle dancing of these small lives, the large scene still seems empty until, glancing up, one realizes that the high, white rocks are moving. They are Dall sheep, grazing slowly across the steep face of the mountain. Or it may be a moose shouldering through the willows that suddenly quickens the landscape. Then the wide land emanates a new and different soul.

The rarer sightings—of lynx and wolverine and wolf—seem like visions, revelations when they do appear, for in these almost mythic animals there is a wilderness quintessence of furtive, predatory grace. I remember arriving at a Noatak

Valley lake with three friends, newcomers to Alaska. When the airplane had left, silence returned, and my friends scanned in awe the emptiness around us. High on the mountainside there was motion, however. Two wolves loped along it, one light gray, the other black. Their long bodies seemed to flow. Like music breaking silence or a star in the night, wild grace had touched the landscape with two small flecks of animal presence and energy, making the land whole, and wholly beautiful.

Sometimes the Brooks Range comes to life in another way, equally wonderful but far more awesome. If it were set to music, that music would be bass, Wagnerian. The unforgettable metamorphosis is the rock or tawny hummock that moves or rises to become bear. Huge bear. Great grizzly bear. One moment one saunters carefree though a beautiful wilderness, appreciative, self-confident, self-possessed. The next moment the same person is a lowly, dreading intruder upon imperial domains, abject before the emperor. There are not many occasions any more for a human being to feel so small, so very weak and humble: in Africa, in the jungle, under the sea, to be sure. A prairie dweller must feel that way before an onrushing tornado. No hiding place, and what to do? We face a thousand likelier dangers: traffic, electricity, mechanical failure, poisons, violence and crime. Yet none produces such primordial, fearful awe as a great fanged beast, indifferent though he may be. The reaction is probably in our very genes.

Except for birdlife in the nesting and migration seasons, most of these animal manifestations are but occasional displays—slight flickerings of movement across the sea of taiga and tundra and its chop of mountain scarps. But twice each year the Brooks Range witnesses a spectacle of animal movement of such magnitude that it ranks among the world's greatest remaining biological events. It is the semiannual migration of the barren-ground caribou.

Fourteen caribou herds spread from western Alaska to Baffin Island. Two of the largest traverse the Brooks Range: the Western Arctic herd of a quarter of a million animals and the Porcupine herd, some two hundred thousand strong. The latter moves between eastern arctic Alaska and Canada's Mackenzie River country, its name derived from the Porcupine River midway in that range. Biologists also recognize between the two herds a smaller Central Arctic herd, probably recruited in part from the two larger flanking ones.

These deer of the north, close relatives of Europe's reindeer and the woodland caribou of eastern Canada, are the remnant of the vast wildlife multitudes that once covered North America more numerously (if not as diversely) than wildlife in Africa. Wildlife biologist George Calef calls them "the central creatures of the

North, the pulse of life in the land." To follow them, he says, is to experience every facet of the northern environment.

"Shaped by the snows of millennia, they are completely at home in the country of winter," he writes in *Caribou and the Barren-Lands*.

> *Theirs are the lands so recently emerged from beneath the snow and glaciers of the great ice age. Over these meagre lands they travel, obeying the commands of the seasons: the melting of snow, the budding of plants, the hatching of mosquitoes, the freeze-up of lakes and rivers. Like the wind that passes over the tundra wilderness and is gone, caribou are forever on the move. They appear on one distant horizon and vanish on the other. And it is their comings and goings that set the cadence of life on the barren lands.*
>
> *The massing of the bison has vanished from the plains; the vast flocks of passenger pigeons that once darkened the sky are gone, never to return. But the majestic herds of caribou move over the tundra today as they always have, submerging the harsh land beneath a tide of life.*

Some biological clock or seasonal manifestation of nature triggers the migratory urge in the gravid cows that paw away the snow to feed in the valleys of the Kobuk, Yukon, and Mackenzie river systems. In early spring, the animals head north toward their ancestral calving grounds. Gaunt and ragged from winter's wear, they trek through the Brooks Range passes, last year's calves often at their sides. They come at last to the plains of their birthing at the period when the cottongrass is budding and most nutritious. Most of the wolves have stopped to den in the hills and birth their own young. The dreaded mosquitoes have not yet hatched. It is the time.

For the great Arctic herd, the calving grounds center around the Utukok River on the western Arctic Slope. The Porcupine herd goes to the eastern part of Alaska's Arctic Coast, a place where oil exploration may now interfere. The cows disperse themselves widely and, within a few days, have dropped their young upon the frozen ground. After a few hours at most, the calves are wobbling after their mothers, grazing as well as nursing, and a vital bond of recognition between mother and offspring is established.

Then the groups gather together. The bulls, which have lingered far behind in the hills, join in the growing aggregation until the herd is a single host, moving across the arctic landscape. The pulse of even a few thousand caribou in a valley can dispel that strange arctic solitude so palpable during most Brooks Range journeys. To witness a herd from the air is to think that the tundra itself is moving. Wilderness

27

guide Bob Waldrop once found himself walking among caribou "as far as the eye could see." "They brushed past us," he recalled. "We were washed along in an ocean of caribou until we began to feel like them."

As Margaret Murie has described the event so beautifully in *Two in the Far North*,

> *The quiet, unmoving landscape . . . had come alive. . . . The rightful owners had returned. Collectively, they make a permeating, uncanny rumble, almost a roar, not to be likened to anything else I can think of. But the total effect of sound, movement, the sight of those thousands of animals, the clear golden western sky, the last sunlight on the mountain slope, gave one a feeling of being a privileged onlooker at a rare performance—a performance in Nature's own way, in the setting of countless ages, ages before man.*
>
> *This was the culmination of all the good things the river and the mountains had already shown us. Here was the living, moving, warm-blooded life of the Arctic—out of some far valley to the west of this region, into some far valley to the east—with the wisdom of the ages, moving always, not depleting their food supply, needing all these valleys and mountains in which to live.*

This was July. The big aggregation had broken up, and the caribou were foraging through the mountains in smaller though still-impressive herds. By September, their aimless wanderings (often frantic flights from the torture of mosquitoes and flies) become purposeful trendings south and east. Herd joins with herd to thread the passes toward lusher pastures of heaths and grasses and lichens—lands where the snow cover is softer than the wind-packed crusts of the north slopes. The animals are in prime now, their gray-brown coats ruffed and streaked with white. The huge antlers of the bulls are polished for the coming battles of the rut.

Lois Crisler watched a herd heading southward up the Killik Valley toward the Continental Divide. "It was a spectacle like none left on Earth now," she wrote in *Arctic Wild*.

> *It had power over the spirit. The power lay not only in what you saw—this slender column driving onward into wilderness. It lay also in what you knew. Arctic night and hunger coming. In-gathering far away of individuals into this traveling column, driven by the great seasons. Knowledge of danger and darkness and fear, built into their*

tissues by the centuries. Life and the cold Arctic before you for a moment in one silent sweep of land and moving animals.

At the end of a masterful story, beautifully photographed in *Caribou and the Barren-Lands,* George Calef writes a message as well as a summary:

> *Barren-ground caribou are creatures of the wilderness and of the ice-age winter. They have survived by the vicissitudes of half a million years. The forces of ice and snow that changed the face of the land shaped and strengthened the caribou. So is man a wilderness creature; we too strove and survived against the ice and the weather, and the change. The wilderness formed our most valued and uniquely human characteristics. One does not destroy the place from which he has sprung except at great peril. Unless we understand these things, we will not do what is right for the caribou, or for ourselves.*

A Kobuk Valley Inupiat woman butchers a caribou. (National Park Service photograph by Robert Belous)

PEOPLE OF THE WEATHER

Time was when all people awoke to wilderness with every rising. For millions of years, hunters and gatherers scanned the land, sky, waters, plants, and animals of each day to learn how to live it appropriately. . . . Humanity's ancient daily dialogue with wild lands was the origin of the wide-ranging consciousness that distinguishes the human species from other creatures.

—Joseph W. Meeker

The Brooks Range is a land aware. It sees you when you come into it, and it watches you throughout your sojourn. It judges you. If you show humility and respect, you may experience some accord. You may never feel comfortable there, few life forms do, except perhaps the Raven, who created it, they say. But you may feel some rapture along with the humility, and closer, somehow, to what the Earth has so long been and meant.

That has been the view of the Native Americans who have lived in and around the Brooks Range for millennia. The land can be shared, so long as you do not regard it as merely something to tread upon. Go softly and carefully, yes, reverently. Do not stare or point at things—at animals or at mountains—or talk about them overly, or be boastful. They do not like it. It is disrespectful, like staring at another person.

31

In Athapaskan and Inupiat tradition, all things are interconnected and have inherent personality and power. Speaking of the Koyukon people in *Make Prayers to the Raven*, Richard K. Nelson has written:

> the environment is like a second society . . . whose blessings are given only to the reverent. . . . Human existence depends on a morally based relationship with the overarching powers of nature. Humanity acts at the behest of the environment. The Koyukon must move with the forces of their surroundings, not attempting to control, master, or fundamentally alter them. They do not confront nature, they yield to it. . . . The Koyukon thus perceive a world in which humanity, nature, and the supernatural are not separated but united within a single cosmos. . . . And binding this conceptual design together is the moral code . . . a single moral order.

As a Koyukon acquaintance of Nelson put it, "The country knows. If you do wrong things to it, the whole country knows. It feels what's happening to it."

And thus, as the country cares, it can be offended, for all things are spiritually invested and have a special, powerful kind of life. Gary Snyder points out in his book *The Practice of the Wild* that "the world is not only watching, it is listening too. A rude and thoughtless remark about a Ground Squirrel or a Flicker or a Porcupine will not go unnoticed."

For the Native people of the Brooks Range, the intimacy of their relationship to nature goes far beyond the ken of western European civilization. Not only is there complete physical dependence on the natural world but there is an emotional interplay as well. Even before modern technology gave western civilization its enormous alterative powers, the western approach to nature was a practical one of manipulation and extraction. For hunter-gatherers worldwide, people who had not the means to alter and harness their environment, the approach was and is essentially propitiatory and religious. Even today, when the people of the Brooks Range have modern tools, ideological restraints remain.

The emotions of the Native people toward their Brooks Range world are somewhat similar to western civilization's veneration of sacred symbols. Their veneration, however, extends to the community of nature itself. Its creatures, its plants, its very rocks and waters, are manifestations of spiritual powers that are conscious, sensate, personified. These must not only be revered but entreated, for there is interdependence between humanity and the rest of its world. The spirit of the land needs the attentions of its people, as a church needs a congregation. The blessings to be expected in return are luck, nature's way of taking care of people. It is not the luck of pure chance, but the reward of skill and patience, and respect.

For those of the Brooks Range, therefore, the terrain is suffused with personal experience, historical tradition, and spiritual insight. Each place is unique and endowed with unseeable dimensions and significance. No one can stand apart. Human separateness is an illusion. That is why the people of the weather do not view as impersonal wilderness a land of which they are an integral part, and to whom each element, however small, has meaning.

Nor is there a logical hierarchy of importance. To the Native people, nothing that lives is humble. Every hunted creature is to be taken as humanely as possible, and thanked for its help in human survival. Even the smallest mouse should be compensated when its food cache is removed for human use. A proper, cordial relationship with animals is vital in maintaining a sense of identity—the sense of how the world functions and how people are to conduct themselves, notes Calvin Martin in *American Indian Environments*. "Animals instruct human beings . . . in the mysteries of life. By giving heed to animals and their ways—by making themselves receptive to their counsel, hunters learn how they must behave." "Other beings . . . do not mind being killed and eaten as food," comments Snyder, "but they expect us to say please, and thank you, and they hate to see themselves wasted."

All creatures are parts of a whole, vast, interconnected society. Indeed, in Athapaskan–Inupiat cosmology, many species were once human themselves, and they have, at least collectively, an immortal soul. The great bear, the wolf, the raven, the omniscient swan have major powers, as one might expect, but so also do the berries, nurtured close to the Earth. And so does the beneficent white spruce, which may never be cut down without a reason.

The establishment of Christianity in Brooks Range communities has produced faithful adherents and significant beneficial social force. It has come to overlie, rather than replace, the world view of the Native people, however. To Brooks Range folk, their Earth is not a vale of tears, a sink of sin, with another world the only hope of happiness and salvation. Nor is it a transcendental world of God-in-nature. It is not a place for introspection, for philosophical speculation, or a place for either religious or aesthetic ecstasy. The Brooks Range inhabitants may note and admire the delicate hues of flowers, the glow of a sunset, the striking beauty of a mountain. They perceive elegance in the land and its life forms much as all people do. A great deal of their sense of beauty, however, derives from the practical admiration of well-doing and well-obtaining. It is in personal and family competence in the real world of the Brooks Range that they find most fulfillment and hope, a world that harbors not satanic terrors but only opportunity and challenge for a full and conscientious career. The trails to the afterlife lead up and down real rivers, where the soul's progress is enjoyably earned.

Human eyes first watched Brooks Range peaks for weather, its passes for game. Even today, seal hunters out on the Chukchi Sea ice are watchful of those westernmost fingers of the range, the Igichuk, Mulgrave, and Lisburne hills. They look for a shimmering, a subtle mirage that makes the hills seem to float, disconnected from their bases. This means that an east wind is beginning to blow from the land, its warmer air acting as a prism to make the mountains levitate. It also means that the wind can blow the ice floes out to sea, kayaks, sleds, hunters, and all.

And people still watch the passes for those first caribou heralding a migrating herd. Far-ranging snow machines and airplanes can now monitor the movements of the herds, but hunters must stand alert for those herd leaders that promise food.

They have been doing this for more than ten thousand years, ever since people first came to the Brooks Range, following the animals that had re-established themselves as the glaciers melted back.

The people came as guests of the land and still regard themselves as such. They came willing to be tested by its stern regime. They passed the test. Generation upon generation, they have continued to pass it, successfully, indeed happily, but also respectfully. They have been courteous and grateful toward the land.

They knew it, know it, by heart—each nubble and creek bend of it, as a farmer knows his fields. It has never been to them the wilderness it came to be in the eyes and minds of modern explorers. To the Native people it was the scene of their livelihood. Rigorous and demanding though it might be, it was home. The land had no other name, but every nook and cranny did—every place where an animal or fish or useful plant might be found, every location of vantage or shelter or spot where an important or interesting event had occurred. In a landscape that might seem repetitive, monotonous, each pool in a river, each grove had special distinction, its uniqueness appreciated by the people and particularly named. They had no maps. They made them in their heads as they went, and could recount the minute details of their travels. And those who heard them remembered. Knowing those details of the landscape was an essential part of hunting, and hunting was life.

Archaeologists are only beginning to learn about the early ages of human occupancy in the Brooks Range, the earliest cultural sites located to date being along the Kobuk River. Many have also been identified at Cape Krusenstern on the Chukchi Sea. Traces of early man have been found deep within the mountains as well, indicating that the whole region has been frequented by human beings over thousands of years.

Forebears of those whom Europeans have called Eskimos moved in from the west and north. They prefer their own designation—Inupiat: "The People," "The Real People." Other groups coming into the Brooks Range country even earlier were the ancestors of the Athapaskan Indians, who migrated from the south and southeast.

Part of the circumpolar Inuit race, the Inupiat were originally coastal folk dependent principally on sea mammals and fish, but they also established themselves along the major west-flowing rivers, the Kobuk and Noatak, where there were good supplies of fish and of land animals and wild plants as well. Timber advanced there as glaciers retreated. The valley Inupiat were in close enough contact with coastal neighbors to trade easily for such marine products as the seal oil important for food and light and cooking.

One group, the Nunamiut, ventured into the heart of the central Brooks Range to become mountain nomads. In legend the Nunamiut were created near the headwaters of the Alatna River by their culture hero, giant Aiyagomahala, who taught them hunting skills. When he left, never to return, he stuck one of his mittens in the ground as a reminder of his teachings. One of the Arrigetch Peaks near the Alatna is a huge mitten-shaped monolith. They were almost entirely dependent on the caribou herds, while obtaining essential supplies of seal oil and other marine resources during summer trading journeys to the Arctic Coast. (In early times, the musk ox also was a source of food, but by 1858 the last indigenous musk ox had been killed. The state has now begun a restocking program.)

In the later 1800s, there may have been as many as a thousand Nunamiut living in and near the Brooks Range. As the century closed, however, a drastic cyclic reduction in the caribou population drove the people to the coast, where wages from the Arctic whaling industry were attractive. By the early twentieth century, whaling had faded, the caribou population was still down, the land having been overhunted to supply whalers, and the Nunamiut were ravaged by disease and liquor. Shamans led one remnant band back to the mountains to escape these influences. When, in the late 1930s, the commercial fur trapping that had sustained many Nunamiut along the coast also degenerated, many more turned to their ancient homeland. Gradually the mountain bands congregated near Anaktuvuk Pass, where the last nomadic family joined them in 1960.

The Athapaskan Indians, meanwhile, lived along tributaries of the Yukon: the Koyukon along the Alatna and Koyukuk; the Gwich'in in the valleys of the Chandalar and Porcupine, in the Porcupine's Sheenjek, Coleen, and Old Crow branches; and in the Mackenzie region as well. Rivers were their geography. These Indians lived in the subarctic forest, subsisting not only on the caribou but also on moose and other game and fish. There is evidence in archaeology and oral history that at times the Indians occupied mountain areas as well. Indeed, names like Itkillik refer to places that Indians frequented. Despite some cautious trading, there were conflicts between the two ethnic groups in the mountains, and by the time the first Caucasians entered the scene, the Indians had moved out of the main ranges. Those remaining in the eastern Brooks continued to make winter trading journeys to the coast, along such traditional routes as the Hulahula and Firth rivers.

Both the Inupiat and the Athapaskans lived in family or multifamily units that often collected in what might be called villages—communities of people related by blood or marriage or hunting partnerships. But change is the norm in a realm that seldom knows stability. Those who live on wild harvests must be always ready to move: with the seasons to hunt or fish or trade, dispersing or regrouping as economic or social needs may dictate. Groups that tended to inhabit a particular valley did become known and named as the people of that area, but territory was not fixed, and there was family interconnectedness far and wide. Having relatives or in-laws in a distant community could mean the difference between hospitality and survival or being attacked as an unwelcome stranger. All other associations were subordinated to the ties of family.

The coming of the Caucasians began to change the old nomadic ways. Missions, churches, trading posts, then schools with mandatory enrollment tended to fix Native residence. More recently, air strips became essential depots where came the heating oil that replaced spruce or willow wood as fuel. There also came the equipment that enabled hunters on snow machines to range far, give up nomadic life, and enjoy modern comforts in permanent villages, with houses built of lumber replacing semisubterranean dwellings of skins and poles and sod.

Both the Inupiat and Athapaskans still regularly go in summer to family fishing camps or in winter to trapping cabins, but, though still widely traveled along rivers or upon snow, by airplane, and in some places by all-terrain vehicles, the Brooks Range is now a land almost empty of habitation. Only Anaktuvuk Pass remains a place of communal settlement in the heart of the mountains. Other Native communities are along the edges of the range, on rivers or on the Arctic Coast.

Yet despite the profound changes that civilization has brought, Inupiat and Athapaskan life remains closely tied, culturally as well as economically, to the rhythms of nature. The Inupiat calendar shows this: January is New Sunshine; February, Icicle Time. March and April mean Hawks Coming, then Geese. May is Ice Breakup Time; June, Birth Time. July is Molting Time, and August is Loose Antler Velvet Time.

September is known as Bird Migration Time. In October come Freezeup Time and Caribou Breeding Time. November is Sunset Time; December, No Sunshine.

The Native people are still basically hunter-gatherers, subsisting on what the wild land offers and forming part of its biological system. Even today, amid a ready food-for-cash economy, the people of a single village will consume a million dollars' worth of wild meat, fish, and plant produce each year.

The term *subsistence* seems to carry with it a sense of perpetual meagerness and hardship: getting by. For the people of the Brooks Range there were certainly many times of starving in the past, before they had rifles. Even thereafter they often went hungry. In older times, when game was scarce or absent, when it required dogteams to find food, and dogs as well as people had to be fed, the people had to hope that a few hares, ground squirrels, fish—and even, in extremis, the faint nourishment in caribou dung—would mean survival.

But there were also many rich feasts. Few people in the world have developed greater skills not only in surviving, but also enjoying, one of Earth's harshest environments. Tireless and self-reliant in their work, inured to pain and suffering, welcoming fright as a honer of skill and fortitude, they celebrated their world and themselves. The hunter's life was their way, their glory, and most modern Native Alaskans still strongly prefer the wild food. They know what it means to their culture as well as to their palates. More than a means of survival, subsistence living is an organized social system of production, distribution, and exchange, forming a complex cultural network of associations, rights, and obligations, of contributions and rewards.

The people of the Brooks Range are people of the weather. It is ever a dominant concern and topic of discussion. Not a querulous one, however, for they take for granted the wind, the cold, the condition of snow. For snow, unless it lies too deep in the subarctic forests, is a facilitator of subsistence living. Among portents of winter are roughened scales of the whitefish, who is "putting on the parka," as the Inupiat say, and they will taste the first snow in welcome. Wind is always a capricious presence, harsh yet helpful to the stalking hunter. This Inupiat grandmother's comment is quoted by psychiatrist Robert Coles in his poetic, moving book *The Last and First Eskimos:* "The wind wants to speak, and we know how to listen. We have survived here because we know how to listen." And as a grandfather explains to Coles, "I must teach our young ones that when the weather sends us signals, we have to pay attention."

As for the cold, the people of the Brooks Range arrived there on a winter's night, as it were, and for them winter is life. Though they must endure its assaults, it means not only mobility and adventure, but also the closeness and sharing that mean happy survival. Moreover, as anthropologist Vilhjalmur Stefansson maintained, the Arctic is basically a friendly place, with food enough for those who know how to cope.

Summer is an interruption, a laxity, troubling psychologically to people who know they were put on Earth to marry winter and enjoy its shadows. In summer's endless glare and swarming insects, the northern peoples feel exposed, losing the condition that keeps a keen edge on the life that is their legacy and pride. They sense that they exist to be tested, and summer does not do that to their satisfaction.

Yet summer is a busy time, when many families like to camp at favorite fishing places. For the river people, however, today as in earlier times, fishing is a primary activity. After a period of quiescence and sometimes scarcity of wildlife in June and July, the salmon and whitefish runs, augmenting resident species, keep everyone busy. The river people know each likely fishing place: in which eddy to seine for salmon or for whitefish, where to find the most pike or burbot, and where the huge, delicious sheefish lie. The alacrity with which they can catch and process fish is legendary: fifty seconds to scale and cut a whitefish, less than three minutes to cut and clean a salmon. Such speed is necessary when human hands must process fish that may come from the nets at a rate (for whitefish) of more than two thousand per hauling. Soon rack after rack of drying fish line the shores. When sled dogs were used extensively, a family might need to catch and dry up to a thousand salmon just for dogfood, for a hard-working twelve-dog team can require nearly forty pounds of food per day—the equivalent of several caribou per week for dogteam and household. (Those few families who still own sled dogs are now more dependent than ever on fish or commercial sources for dogfood; Alaskan law forbids using caribou for dogfood.)

Summer is also, of course, the time for berrying, digging the *masu,* the "Eskimo potato," and gathering other wild plants. Each good gathering ground is known despite all the seeming sameness of the land, and each family has its favorite sites. In some ways, the northern people have been as dependent upon vegetation as on meat and fish. Athapaskans have always looked to their forest environment for fuel, and haul firewood much of the year. Inland Inupiat north of the forests had to use willow, and a large household might need to burn fifty pounds or more per day of the scarce shrub.

As men today often seek employment away from home, the best Kobuk hunters in earlier summertimes went away for most of the season, hiking deep into the mountains with pack dogs to find sheep, caribou, marmot, and bear. They had

A musher helps his sled dogs pull up from the frozen Anaktuvuk River. (National Park Service photograph by the author)

to eat most of the meat themselves, but still brought back heavy loads of hides, sinew, dried meat, and fat. Mountain people, the Nunamiut, on the other hand, went to the coast for fishing and trading.

Although they are usually thought of as sled people, Brooks Range inhabitants have been among the world's greatest hikers, walking or snowshoeing on journeys as long as two hundred miles. Hunting parties often covered thirty miles in a day. To walk for frigid days through deep snow with neither tent nor sleeping bag was thought to be no great achievement. One villager is recorded to have walked sixty-five miles for some tobacco. As dog-mushing developed, distances of fifty miles a day could be covered with two- to three-hundred-pound sledloads. Now snow machines speed over even greater distances in a day. Occasionally, hunters use aircraft.

Augusts of old saw hunters returning with packs so heavy that they sometimes needed staffs to steady themselves over the hummocky ground. When possible, they rafted down rivers toward home. Reed River in the central Brooks Range was known as Anitgaakgaak, "The Going Home Way."

In late summer, the first caribou filter through Brooks Range passes, and the great fall hunt begins. The animals are in prime condition then, after a summer on the Arctic Slope. The bulls are fat and have splendid hides, and are the preferred quarry until they smell of the rut. Then plump cows are chosen.

In the times before firearms, the Inupiat constructed vast corralling devices that could funnel a herd into a pond or stone pen where they could be speared or shot with arrows. Stone monuments called *inuksuks,* resembling human figures, were ranged across the tundra in a long *V* formation, augmented by as many real

39

people as possible. Shying from these, the herd drove forward and into the trap. The last such great cooperative caribou-catching occurred in 1944. Travelers in the Brooks Range occasionally come across inuksuks still commanding the barren ridges somewhat like the standing stones of ancient Britain and France.

The occasional caribou drive did not lessen the need for skill at stalking or ambush at which hunters had to succeed even in the dead of winter, when caribou are particularly wary. Like hunting peoples elsewhere, their sensitivity in tracking game was so great that a master hunter could follow bear tracks in frozen moss covered by thick, undisturbed snow.

With firearms came new hunting skills to equal the accurate arrow and the spear braced against a bear's lungs. For example, hunters refrained from killing the caribou leading the herd lest it turn; they shot animals on the far side of the migrating herd to reduce the danger of its stampeding away. So skillful was their aim that the killing of grizzly bears with .22-caliber rifles is recorded. Ammunition was precious, and a man with ten or twenty cartridges was deemed wealthy. Ever wary of emergencies, hunters never expended all the ammunition they had with them. Often they loaded their cartridges with gunpowder sufficient to kill yet leave the bullet within the animal for reuse.

Although prestigious, physically challenging, and the stuff of many stories, hunting grizzly bear was considered easy. The huge animals were most often killed in their dens. If encountered in the open, they were goaded to impale themselves upon a held spear, or outmaneuvered and shot. Use of dogs lessened the danger and enabled hunters to place small-caliber shots with precision. He who had the skill and endurance to pursue the intelligent wolf was the most committed, respected hunter of all.

For the Athapaskans, the preeminent moose hunters, the fall moose hunt has always been a major event, and ever a principal topic of conversation. Virtually every adult male, as well as many teen-age boys and women, actively participate in the hunting. The waning of autumn lends urgency to the hunt, for without a moose, a family may have to rely on commercial meats or the charity of others.

Inasmuch as hunter-gatherers must exploit all food resources at hand, the arrival of migratory waterfowl has always been welcomed as well as the ptarmigan that move seasonally through the range in large flocks. Trapping and snaring, of course, have also been integral parts of the hunting life. Earlier in this century, commercial fur trapping gave Native people needed cash, but selling pelts has ceased to be a significant activity. Much trapping continues for personal use of pelts and meat, however.

Until modern times, which have brought a weakening of the old respect for the prey, hunters did not indulge in reckless killing. Preferring to call it "catching," they took no pleasure in the death-dealing itself, for there was a mythic, cordial bond between hunter and hunted. The joy of hunting was in the stalk and the accurate shooting, the quick-mindedness and agility, and the knowledge that the hunters' own lives and those of their families would be sustained.

In modern times, the snow machine has become the great equalizer among hunters, but at the cost of some traditional environmental and physical skills, as well as ethics. The snow machine also has caused some breakdown of communication between generations. The youth of today do not hunt as often as their grandfathers did in close association with older, more experienced hunters. The importance of hunting traditionally encouraged a rapport between the young and the older, making hunting a means of passing on knowledge and philosophy from one generation to another. But money and its power to buy private transportation make the young no longer so dependent upon the village sages and their traditional knowledge, skill, and attitudes. Mandatory school attendance, of course, also prevents teen-agers from getting outdoor experience with their elders.

Even as long ago as 1917, Archdeacon Hudson Stuck, the intrepid dog musher-clergyman who founded the Episcopal mission of St. John's-in-the-Wilderness at Allakaket, advised that "the wise teacher, the wise missionary, will not seek to keep boys at school who should be out in the woods serving their apprenticeship." An old chief specially thanked him for a sermon in which he preached:

> *Reading and writing are good things, and the other things the school teaches are good things, and that is why we put the school here to teach them, but knowing how to make a living on the river or in the woods, winter and summer, is a much better thing, a very much more important thing, and something that the school cannot teach and the fathers must. Let us have both if we can, but whatever happens don't let your boys grow up without learning to take care of themselves and of their wives and children by and by.*

For the people of the weather, the homemaking skills, however transient that home might be, are married to those of the hunter-gatherer. As flexibility and innovation are keys to survival, gender roles adapt to changing situations. Although hunting has usually been the activity most appropriate for men, much outdoor as well as indoor work has always been done by women. Athapaskan and Inupiat women are often excellent hunters, avidly sharing hunting pleasures with their spouses. They are likely to do most of the fishing and fish processing, and much of the small game hunting, for their husbands are frequently away on big-game hunts or earning wages. And, when necessary, women are quite capable of taking on the total hunting responsibility in addition to being the pillars of an incredibly busy home life. So crucial is the partnership of husband and wife in subsistence living that a widow or widower has a hard time, and must either remarry or seek family assistance.

Women produce most of the goods on which family life depends: the nets, the baskets, the leather, the garments. Sewing is perhaps the supreme, most crucial, skill, which ensures that skin boats do not leak and that moccasins and parkas are durable protection against the rigors of outdoor life.

For a boy, to become a man has meant to become a hunter. First working with his elders and then on his own, a boy reaches his hunting reputation by his late teens. Girls, likewise, are expected to absorb the expertise and lore needed to fulfill their role in maturity: to be primarily responsible for household activities. Throughout their teens, they gradually perfect their sewing skills, but the necessity for excellent sewing is so great that a woman may be thirty years old before she is considered really accomplished. Good sewing is so important for survival that boys also are instructed in how to repair boots or mittens.

Among the people of the weather, young couples do not manifest romantic attitudes. Affectionate in more subtle ways, they strengthen their bonds as children arrive and the family becomes more and more an integral part of the community. Crucial to a successful marriage are hard work, faithfulness, and avoidance of criticism. Couples must live so constantly in such close quarters that privacy is much respected. Men's hunting together and women's visiting together give respite that enables each gender better to tolerate the other in the otherwise perpetual proximity of their married lives.

The families of the Brooks Range are generally large ones, with children not only much loved but also needed. Without a daughter, a woman has no one to help with the countless home chores. A man needs a son to join him on the hunts and to maintain the sleds or boats. Relatives work closely together, and close working partnerships between men or between women are often formed. Children, though indulged when young, learn early on the roles expected of them: the sharing of the family's and community's chores. The village children will take care of a family's elder members if the active adults are too busy or are away. Children's play is usually imitative of their parents' daily activities of the season, and covert instruction turns play into training. By the time she is eight, a girl is of substantial help in the home, and boys of that age are assisting their fathers with the equipment repairs. By the time they are eleven, the boys are learning to hunt big game.

In his 1951 book on the Nunamiut of Anaktuvuk Pass, Helge Ingstad wrote this delightful vignette of the village children:

> They are mountain children, these—with deep, wide chests and powerful limbs and aglow with vitality. At three years old they dash up the hillsides like goats. At seven they can run for a long time without getting tired. They are like animals in their sensitive alertness and swift reactions. And they are sharp. They play with stones, sand, sticks, and bones and have tremendous fun with them. They form teams and play old Eskimo games, rush about trying to catch one another, and nearly pull the tents down. They are never bored, but are fully occupied all day long until they drop down to sleep among the caribou skins in the evening.
>
> Children are regarded as wealth. One thing is that they make a home and that their parents are fond of them, but what is just as important is that children secure their parents' future by giving them help while growing up and in later life.

In a culture wherein self-reliance, self-control, and persistence are expected, where sorrow is sublimated and adversity accepted with equanimity, one's prestige derives from the good performance of what is expected. Hospitality, sharing, and readiness to give help when needed are traits also honored as characteristic of the culture. If a man does not share, it may be said that "he is trying to act like a white man." Inupiat and Athapaskans do not allow individuals to think only of themselves.

The Native people of the Brooks Range region, like so many elsewhere, have not been allowed to maintain their old societal harmonies and the almost blood relationship with the land and its creatures. Caucasian culture has moved in. As an Inupiat woman remarked to Robert Coles,

> The winds from the lower forty-eight [are] blowing hard, and bringing not snow or rain, but all of the white people's toys and tricks and ideas! . . . Their planes fly over us. Their boats come by us. Their music won't let us sleep. Their potato chips and Coca-Cola are as bad as their alcohol. We have become their slaves.
>
> The white people, I am afraid to say, won't let people just stay as they are. . . . They want more than anything else for us to think like them! And they are getting their way—in everything, they are. That is true!

Such acculturation began in the early nineteenth century, of course, when trade goods began arriving, but at first the new tools had little effect except to make life somewhat more assured. With the twentieth century, however, came the missionaries, then the schools and their gravitational force toward settled living and its attendant health problems. Alcohol, the scourge of Native American peoples since earliest colonial times, often brought such rampant problems that some villages banned it, albeit often with only partial success. A doctor in Kotzebue during the 1970s once remarked that every health problem in that Native center, from broken limbs to freezing, was alcohol-related.

Television is supplanting the old traditions of visiting and storytelling, turning the Native people into "tubivores." Settled living also means depletion of subsistence resources nearby. It means need for cash to buy the equipment and fuel required to go farther and farther to hunt, fish, and trap—equipment that in places is hurting the land. Moreover, the wild world of the Brooks Range and its environs now knows radar and oil rigs, mining camps, sport hunters and tourists. Its space is destroyed by airplanes, snow machines, and all-terrain vehicles, many of them sought and used by the Natives themselves. Practical people, they use what technology offers, increasingly oblivious, it would seem, to the wounding of their homeland. Anaktuvuk Pass, once just a good hunting place where firewood was available, has become an oil-fueled, oil-subsidized metropolis, transportation hub for cross-country machinery.

With the Alaska Native Claims Settlement Act of 1971, America attempted in a single legal stroke to transform an ancient subsistence society, and bring it into mainstream corporate life. As a result, Native corporations that own vast tracts surrounding or extending into the federal and state holdings have tended to bring briefcase leadership to a culture that had revered local consensus, the chief's hunting judgment, and the shaman's propitiatory arts. For many an average Native Alaskan of the north, wages have replaced caribou as something to be taken when opportunity arises, with the "meat" of cash laid up to fulfill a family's needs until a job again appears. There are few economic opportunities to replace subsistence, however, which remains a cultural imperative. But now the wildlife on which self-sufficiency relies is becoming more circumscribed, both by competing interests and by regulation. Subsistence has always been assumed to be a dynamic enterprise, fitted to circumstances; now it is being more closely defined and limited lest it compete with other needs and sovereignties. Direst of all possibilities is the specter of corporate takeovers that could rob the people of their land.

Many subsistence people in Alaska are trying to conduct their corporate business in traditional, consensual ways that go far beyond fiscal years and bottom lines and look at long-term wholeness. However, they are not immune to the temptation of commercialism. Again and again wisdom must wrestle with greed. Wisdom often loses.

The secret to life in the north is and always has been adaptability, self-sufficiency. The Native people of the region have been able to return to subsistence living when the dollar economy has slackened. But what if the dynamism of subsistence, eight-wheeled, perhaps, is too sophisticated, too destructive, and the wildlife resources dwindle? There seem to be no tidy solutions, yet the Athapaskans and Inupiat are determined to be themselves, with their own distinct place in contemporary Alaskan and national life, remaining true to their culture as part of the ecosystem and not strangers in the wilderness.

The future seems bleak for the people of the weather, stretched as they are between modern-world demands and temptations that would seem to mock their culture-preserving desires. But National Park Service historian William E. Brown offers words of hope for a society coping with the daily dilemma of living in both a modern and a traditional world, facing external threats to its homeland and disintegrative forces within:

> *The history of these people is a history of survival. For generations and millennia they have proved their steadfastness in a demanding environment... they have seen wave after wave of outsiders come into their world, extract something from it, and leave. Traditionalists are confident that the current inundation—largely oil-and-mineral based; partly sport-and-recreation based—is similarly transient, at least as a major disruptive force. Their sense is that as long as environmental wisdom and sociocultural equity are guides to the future, they can survive this wave also.*

If Brown's hope is true, the people of the weather will preserve for all of us what ecologist Joseph W. Meeker has called "the special form of consciousness that awakens to read the messages written in every wilderness day." Those people, he reminds, "are not relics of a forgotten past, but fully modern human beings coping with contemporary reality.... They have at least two gifts that most people have lost: most understand deeply their relationship to wild land, and they honor the remembrance of their past. Their task, and ours, is to discover how these treasures can combine to form a future."

Ernest de Koven Leffingwell and sled dogs rest at the door of his headquarters on Flaxman Island. The house was built of lumber salvaged from his expedition's sailing vessel. (U.S. Geological Survey photograph by J. B. Mertie)

Philip Smith and J. B. Mertie's Geological Survey expedition of 1924 heads up the Alatna River toward the Killik with eight sleds and teams, hauling canoes in March for a summer's work on the Arctic Slope. (U.S. Geological Survey photograph by J. B. Mertie)

EXPLORATION

The wild requires that we learn the terrain, nod to all the plants and animals and birds, ford the streams and cross the ridges, and tell a good story when we get back home.

—Gary Snyder

The western hills of the Brooks Range, watched for so many generations by Inupiat sealers, were first scanned by Caucasian eyes in 1778. The redoubtable Captain James Cook of the British Royal Navy pushed farther north than had earlier, Russian-sponsored navigators. On August 14, he saw the Mulgrave Hills, "destitute of wood," and, on August 21, named Cape Lisburne, the westernmost extremity of the range, probably for the Earl of Lisburne. He was ten leagues away, but thought that it "appeared to be pretty high land, even down to the sea."

Another British officer, Captain Frederick William Beechey, climbed the cape on August 21, 1826, and gave us the first description of Brooks Range tundra-walking: "The stones were covered with a thick swampy moss, which we traversed with great difficulty, and were soon wet through by it. Vegetation was, however, as luxuriant as in Kotzebue Sound, more than a hundred miles to the southward." Beechey seems to have been the first of the explorers to encounter Brooks Range wildlife: "Several reindeer were feeding on this luxuriant pasture; the cliffs were covered with birds; and the swamps generated myriads of moskitos."

Beechey's climb up Cape Lisburne was not a first Brooks Range ascent, however. On July 21, Sir John Franklin, the naval captain whom Beechey was intending to meet along the Arctic coast, had climbed in the western Buckland Hills. Franklin, too, received and recorded a first taste of what it is like to tramp the tundra. "Though its distance was not more than twelve miles from the coast, the journey proved to be very fatiguing, owing to the swampiness of the ground between the mountain and the sea. We had also the discomfort of being tormented the whole way by myriads of mosquitoes." Apparently, the trip was worth the trouble, for Franklin added, "The view into the interior possessed the charm of novelty, and attracted particular regard. We commanded a prospect over three ranges of mountains ... the view was bounded by a fourth range of high peaked mountains for the most part covered with snow." Franklin's party talked of exploring the high peaks while their vessels were icebound, but they dared not miss an opening in the pack ice that would allow them to proceed.

Sir John seems to have been the first Caucasian to view the full splendor of this arctic cordillera. He called the chain the Rocky Mountains, and, topographically, they do indeed form the northwestern extremity of North America's Rocky Mountain system. At Kay Point, Franklin noted: "Lieutenant Black sketched the beautiful scenery afforded by a view of the Rocky Mountains, while I was employed in collecting specimens of the plants in flower. We now discovered that the Rocky Mountains do not form a continuous chain but that they run in detached ranges at unequal distances from the coast." Franklin named the first high range the British Mountains. Near the end of his voyage—at Flaxman Island—he noted the loftiest chain in the Brooks, which he named in honor of Count Nicholas Romanzof, Russian chancellor and a patron of art and science.

In 1854, another British naval officer, Captain Richard Collinson, set out to climb the Romanzofs. From the coast, he headed toward the Canning River and ascended a steep face, but "getting enveloped in a mist, we were brought to a standstill on a narrow shelf." Seeing peaks to the east and west and a precipitous south slope, Collinson surmised the range to be very narrow. Probably he had merely climbed the first of the outlying ridges, the Sadlerochits.

An American viewed distant snowy Brooks Range summits from the south even before Alaska had been purchased by his country. In 1865, Robert Kennicott, leader of a team sent to find a telegraph route across North America to Siberia, explored the Koyukuk River country from Nulato on the Yukon. He searched northward for a pass that might be used for the route, but "nothing was seen but continuous ranges of snow-covered mountains rolling one over the other for God knows how many miles."

The first official U.S. penetrations into Brooks Range country, like those of Britain, were military. Except for an approach in 1883 from the north—up the Meade River by a scientific-minded army officer, First Lieutenant Patrick Ray—the probes came from the west and south. In rival expeditions of 1884 and 1885–1886, Lieutenant J. C. Cantwell of the Revenue Marine (later the U.S. Coast Guard) and Lieutenant George M. Stoney of the U.S. Navy explored and mapped the Kobuk and Noatak rivers and the Jade Mountains, and pushed across the Arctic Divide.

Cantwell reported hearing of a large lake at the Kobuk's head from which portages might be made to the Colville River. Whaling had been established along the Arctic Coast since the 1850s, and there might be an inland route by which to help the oft-stricken whalers.

Cantwell and Stoney took steam launches as far as they could up the Kobuk River, burning local coal as well as wood, then resorted to skin boats. On his second journey, Cantwell reached the big lake he considered the source of the Kobuk. He called it by its Inupiat name, Car-loog-ah-look-atah, or Big Fish Lake. Stoney referred to this name in a different spelling, but then called it Walker Lake, reportedly for a member of his command. Native mythology populated the lake with fish so large that one leaped out to petrify into the fish-tailed summit of Mount Igikpak. One member of Cantwell's party tried to catch such a monster by baiting a caribou antler with a goose. The fish they did see and catch caused Cantwell to comment: "Were not this report intended as a plain statement of facts coming under my observation, I would hardly dare state what the size of some of the trout we captured was found to be, for fear of being suspected of exaggeration." The trout ran up to three and a half feet in length, and Cantwell reported seeing much larger ones.

Cantwell became the first non-Native to brave Brooks Range rapids on the upper Kobuk (which he called the Kowak). He seems to have been a careless camper, however, for his party started a tundra blaze that consumed "acres and acres" before it burned out. He also seems to have been the first practitioner of "Kilroyism" in the Brooks: he carved his initials and the date on a rock face above the lake.

Apparently the first Alaskan explorer to comment with interest on permafrost, Cantwell was amazed to see lenses of subterranean ice exposed when the Kobuk River's banks eroded, and to realize how thin a mantle of soil supported dense thickets, luxuriant ground cover, even tree groves atop the icy ground.

He wrote engagingly, and his accounts of Kobuk scenery are appreciative:

> *The river suddenly widened to half a mile, and both banks were low and green in the sunshine, while beyond and partly hidden by a light mist a range of rugged mountains could be seen, lying cool and tranquil in the distance.... The sides of the hills were dotted with many species of wildflowers, and under the pines the moss-covered ground was like velvet to the touch.*

"We would have called it Utopia," Cantwell added, "had not the mosquitoes nearly driven us wild." Later, he reported further on that matter: "The mosquitoes were worse than ever, and some of our party were almost unrecognizable from the effects of these pests. It is no uncommon thing to see a man who has been cutting wood . . . suddenly drop his ax and run frantically for the river, his face and hands covered with blood."

On another occasion, Cantwell wrote: "A slight relief was obtained by covering all exposed parts of the body with a thick varnish made of tar, gum arabic, and olive oil; but even with this disagreeable preventive our sufferings were simply indescribable."

Both Cantwell and Stoney made reconnaissance trips to the mysterious Jade Mountains, whence came the beautiful hard green nephrite long prized by Native people for implement blades. The jade occurs as large boulders, but the serpentine rock of the mountains gives them a greenish hue, and the explorers thought the whole mass might be jade. Accounts of the two Cantwell expeditions, one by Assistant Engineer S. B. McLenegan and the other by Cantwell himself, give a vivid description of the hardships involved. "They were in a terribly exhausted condition," Cantwell wrote of McLenegan and a miner companion. "They had been drenched by the rain and tormented by the mosquitoes ever since leaving the river, and their condition was now really pitiable. Their boots had been worn out by hard walking, and they were compelled to cut pieces from their blankets to bind around their feet. Their clothes were torn and their faces, haggard and blood-stained."

Then Cantwell himself made the trip and experienced what it is like to cross taiga country in summer. "Our walk across to the mountain was attended by excessive fatigue," he wrote.

> Our way led across the soft, yielding tundra through lagoons, around lakes and dense thickets of tangled willows and cottonwood, and long stretches of pine [spruce] woods, where fallen trees caused us constantly to turn aside and travel by a circuitous route. At one moment exposed to the burning heat of the summer sun, and the next floundering, plunging, and struggling waist deep in dark pools of stagnant water where the light of day never penetrates, we reached at last the banks of a roaring torrent which sweeps around the base of the Jade Mountain.

They reported the average temperature that day, like many others, at ninety degrees.

W hile Cantwell and his Native-assisted party were winding up the Kobuk for the second time, during the summer of 1885, McLenegan was exploring the next great river to the north, the Noatak. Unable to hire a guide from among the uninformative local people, McLenegan went with but one companion, a seaman named Nelson, on what he termed "a desperate venture."

For twenty-eight days in July, and for some three hundred miles up that swift and often swollen river, they paddled, occasionally sailed, but mostly dragged an Aleutian skin bidarka. It was twenty-seven feet long, with a two-foot beam and three circular hatches in the decked hull, a craft with which the Natives at Hotham Inlet declared it would be impossible to navigate the swift, shallow Noatak.

McLenegan and Nelson were certain they took that boat up the Noatak for five hundred miles. By turns they dragged it, one in the tracking harness, the other manning a steering paddle. Often pelted by rain, they had to wade whenever there was no shoreline footing, and to manhandle the boat through rapids. McLenegan wrote:

> *We had been in water waist deep at times during the greater portion of the day, and consequently before nightfall became thoroughly chilled with the cold. After going into camp for the night our chilled blood, again put in circulation, produced a most peculiar burning sensation, which caused no little pain and utterly precluded the idea of sleep.*

McLenegan recalled that he "oftentimes became so benumbed with cold as to be incapable of motion," and he reported later that "the icy cold water of the river through which we were frequently obliged to drag the canoe, together with the extreme inclemency of the weather, was sufficient to break down the strongest constitution." Reading the report, one can only wonder why they did not die of hypothermia. Perhaps they had not heard of it.

They capsized on the second day and later as well, damaging provisions, which seem to have consisted mostly of flour, bacon, and coffee. They went up blind channels. Their boots wore thin. Native sealskin boots they brought along as spares softened to uselessness in the water, and McLenegan reported that their feet became so painful that "it was difficult to stand upon them." Later, they lost their boots entirely and fashioned rude sealskin moccasins which they strapped on.

But they cached part of their food and stubbornly continued their journey, through the forest lands and the Noatak's Grand Canyon to the treeless tundra above. The rain seemed incessant, which may explain their not mentioning the torment of mosquitoes.

Despite hardship after hardship, and though lacking Cantwell's flair for expression, McLenegan could yet be appreciative of some of the Noatak scenery. As they approached the mountains flanking the Noatak's Grand Canyon, he wrote:

> *The entire range, from base to summit, was of a light red color and destitute of all vegetation, save a fringe of green around the base. The beautiful contrast afforded by snow-capped summits, red slopes, and green bases formed one of the most novel and interesting sights in the entire country and offered a study well worthy of an artist's brush.*

"Nature indeed is very beautiful in those wild desolate regions," he recorded later after seeing a bull caribou, "and I shall never forget the thrill of pleasure experienced as I stood gazing at that wild and untamed creature." After climbing a hill to examine the country, McLenegan wrote:

> *On gaining the eminence, I discovered several small lakes, none of which were more than a mile in length, and situated as they were, walled in by the mountains, their calm and unruffled waters presented an indescribably beautiful appearance, and the peaceful scene on that beautiful Sunday did much to soften the hardships which had attended our way.*

But he could not find beauty in the upper river's tundra basin, swept by a bitter wind. "Before us lay the level plains of the interior, stretching away in the distance, unrelieved by a single object upon which the eye could rest with any feeling of pleasure," he reported, and admitted that the sense of loneliness was "depressing in the extreme."

Nelson finally became ill. McLenegan was dunked in the river thrice in one day, trying to drag the boat through rapids singlehandedly, and pitched camp, chilled to the bone, as rain came on. The boat was now dangerously worn, the river scarcely navigable. They went overland for another day through a torrent of rain and sleet, "obliged to wade through the half-frozen moors." From a hill McLenegan viewed a scene of "utter desolation. . . . The Noatak, no longer the stately river which flowed into the sea, had degenerated into a mere rambling creek," he reported, and added, "As I stood on the height, pelted by the storm and chilled by the fierce Arctic blasts, my thoughts turned back to the home of other days. The fearful contrast of the scene before me and the other, so distinctly pictured on the pages of memory, left no room for expression."

Judging from the map in McLenegan's report, he and Nelson must have gotten somewhere between the Aniuk River and Atongarak Creek. Upriver, there are some braidings and other tributaries that could make the main river appear to end. Actually, it continues on for more than one hundred navigable miles. To journey into the headwaters mountains would have proved little, however, for the two explorers were not equipped to find a route out of the upper valley. In view of the river's condition, that of the boat, and their state of body and mind, they wisely decided to retreat.

And just in time. Heavy storms descended, the river rose three feet, and the two raced for the cache. It was a wild ride, fraught with frantic efforts to avoid rocks lurking beneath the floodwaters. According to McLenegan's calculations, they made an incredible 125 miles in one long, long day of all-out exertion, fearing that they would be too late to save their cache from flood, or would miss it in the inundated landscape. Water was washing through the willow clump where they had left the provisions when they spotted their cache at last, grabbed branches as the current swept them by, and enjoyed a hearty meal again. The long race, said McLenegan, had both figuratively and literally "saved our bacon."

Through all the travails of his journey, McLenegan made geographical observations he seldom mentions, and he made a map. I have compared that map with modern ones drafted with the benefit of aerial photography. His map matches them almost perfectly!

The U.S. Army as well as the Revenue Marine and U.S. Navy was on the march in arctic Alaska in the 1880s. Lieutenant Ray's reconnaissance up the Meade River in 1883 had noted a low range of mountains to the south. Possibly he saw the De Long Mountains, but probably what he saw were merely the low ridges north of the Colville River. Then, while the two marine services were probing the western reaches of the Brooks Range, the Army took a "first look" at it from the south. Lieutenant Henry T. Allen worked his way up the Koyukuk River to its confluence with the John. It was the final stage in an amazing 1,500-mile journey through unknown and supposedly hostile country where previous efforts had failed, a project hailed as the most significant journey of exploration in North America since Lewis and Clark trekked across the western United States to the Pacific Ocean. Alaska historian Morgan Sherwood has called it "the most spectacular individual achievement in the history of Alaskan inland exploration." Allen's abilities would later make him commander of a World War I army division, and of the U.S. Occupation Forces in Germany, following the Armistice.

Interestingly, Sherwood has noted also that Allen's achievement gained little public recognition because Americans did not realize at that time how much unknown territory still existed in North America. "Their attention had been diverted to exploration in Africa, and that so large a segment of their own continent had just been explored for the first time was to many inconceivable. Alaska was an anachronism that the popular mind never fully understood."

After pushing up the huge, glacial Copper River to the Tanana and Yukon, living at times on hares and rotten moose meat, Allen's energy took him on into the land of the "treacherous" Koyukons. With a single companion, Private Frederick W. Fickett, plus some guides, porters, and pack dogs, Allen walked 120 miles to the Kanuti, floated that by canoe for ninety miles to the Koyukuk, and then poled upriver. They reconnoitered the Alatna River at a high clay bank called by the Native people Unatlotly. Allen named the river the Allenkaket (*kaket* meaning river in the Koyukon tongue), a name that stuck to the village where the Episcopal mission of Saint John's-in-the-Wilderness came to stand. Then on they went to the Ascheeshna, which Allen called the Fickett River, later to be named the John.

"We ascended Mount Lookout to get, if possible, the general course of the rivers and mountains," he noted August 8, 1885.

> *From its summit, about 800 to 1,000 feet above the river, we obtained a splendid view of the valley of the Ascheeshna and the mountains in which it rises. The extreme mountains whence it comes appeared to be 60 to 80 miles from us in a right-line course. The highest peaks I should judge are about 4,000 feet high and are snow-covered one-third the distance to their bases.*

As the army's Lieutenant Allen was looking up the John River toward the distant white summits of the Brooks Range, the navy's Lieutenant Stoney was preparing to explore them in depth from the upper Kobuk. The Revenue Marine's Cantwell and McLenegan had gotten farther by boat, but now Stoney had requested and received orders to lead a well-organized party of seventeen officers and enlisted men, winter over, and explore with dogteams. (Stoney considered himself the first Caucasian to have reconnoitered the Kobuk, which he called the Putnam in honor of Charles F. Putnam, U.S.N., who had lost his life in a fire aboard ship in Alaska waters. Stoney proudly reported on his varied and difficult expeditions as having been accident-free.)

The navy men spent the late summer of 1885 obtaining fish for their thirty-six dogs and building a comfortable winter house a few miles downriver from the present-day village of Shungnak. They called it Fort Cosmos, after a club in San Francisco of which the officers were members. On December 1, their journey began. Stoney, Ensign W. L. Howard, and four Natives went north up a major tributary to the Kobuk that the Inupiat called Nutvuktowoark but that Stoney named in honor of a navy surgeon, James M. Ambler. They laid saplings across thin ice and portaged up the steep south face of Nakmaktuak Pass, "the place where gear must be carried," visited the uppermost village then occupied on the Noatak, and proceeded over the Arctic Divide to the Colville Watershed.

In late February, 1886, Stoney, with an interpreter and two other Natives, mushed up the Kobuk through heavy snows and over to the Alatna. They visited what must be Iniakuk Lake (calling it Takahula), proceeded up the Alatna and its tributary Kutuk River to the Arctic Divide and on to Chandler Lake, named by Stoney for Secretary of the Navy William E. Chandler.

The first description of the spectacular Arrigetch Peaks comes from Stoney's pen:

> *They appear in every conceivable way and shape: there are rugged, weather-scarred peaks, lofty minarets, cathedral spires, high towers and rounded domes; with circular knobs, flat tops, sharp edges, serrated ridges and smooth backbones. These fantastic shapes form the summits of bare, perpendicular mountains.*

The winter's expeditions also included a trip by Ensign M. L. Reed up the river and to the hot spring that now bears his name. The most extended, daring, and celebrated reach of the Stoney exploration, however, was Ensign Howard's ninety-six-day trek by sled and, later, boat from Fort Cosmos to Point Barrow. With a seaman named C. M. Price, an interpreter, and two other Natives, plus a backup team as far as the Noatak, he crossed the Arctic Divide, went down the Etivluk River to the Colville, and thence via the Ikpikpuk to the coast.

Howard's terse accounts are the bones of an exciting narrative. He camped in snowdrifts, suffered from snow blindness, and later treated Natives similarly stricken. He was willing to rely largely on Native foods, in spite of which he records losing more than half his body weight. His diplomacy carried him through tribal frontiers to strange villages, and he weathered encounters when tribute was demanded and he suspected that he was being considered a prisoner.

Howard, who became a rear admiral after distinguished service in the Spanish-American War and World War I, witnessed on his journey the twilight of the old-style hunter-gatherers. The next expedition found few Inupiat in the interior.

With a decline in the caribou population and the trend for people to gather into permanent villages, the seasonal communities that Howard and Stoney visited vanished. Save for roving hunters and trappers, fish camps on the rivers, and, later, the settlement at Anaktuvuk Pass, the Brooks Range became an unpeopled land.

New people were coming to its marches, however. In the last flameout of the arctic whaling era, the whaling ships began to overwinter at Herschel Island at the mouth of the Firth River, so as to remain longer on the hunt. A number of whaling captains brought their wives along. One of them, Viola (Mrs. John A.) Cook, spent more than a decade of winters there, enjoying the time until a last, emergency winterover. After receiving photographs of grandchildren she might never see, her mental health broke down.

Wanting fresh meat, the whalers bought much from local hunters, not only Inupiat but also Athapaskan, who traveled to trade from as far as the Porcupine and Peel rivers. Some of the more adventuresome crewmen took to mushing and hunting themselves. "It is truly remarkable how many trips the boat-steerer Peterson has made with sled during the winter, and the amount of meat he has brought in with his teams," wrote Captain Cook. "Living constantly in the country or on the trail, he seems as fresh and healthy as when he started out last fall." Cook recounted on another occasion that "Peterson arrived with 320 pounds of meat from 100 miles up Herschel Island River [the Firth]. . . . He reports the natives made a big killing of deer near the source of the river."

The whalers' need for fresh meat must have impacted Brooks Range wildlife heavily. In one account, Cook noted Peterson's arrival with fifty saddles of mountain sheep. A month later, he was back with fifty-six more. Native hunters supplied far greater quantities of both caribou and sheep, as well as birds. In 1905–1906, five unprepared vessels were forced to spend the winter frozen in at Herschel Island, and fresh meat saved the crews not only from starvation but also from the dreaded scurvy. Cook reported that more than fifty thousand pounds of deer (caribou) meat was brought in, and that there were no deaths and little sickness during that trying time.

Cook had nothing but praise for the charity and self-sacrifice of the Native people who helped the whalers. "The natives were using their own dogs and their own supplies to keep us from starvation, knowing full well that we were powerless to pay them for their work or resupply them with guns, dogs, and ammunition, which they were using for us, unless our sled got through to Eagle City," he wrote in *Pursuing the Whale*, his autobiography, published in 1926, of a quarter-century's whaling.

The natives, knowing this and the chances that they were
sacrificing their all and all that was in them for us, never made a
murmur or for a moment wavered. To that self-sacrificing race it was
enough to know that we needed their help, and it was given as freely as
though gold was glittering before their eyes as their reward. Such
voluntary service and cheerfulness did those natives give the whalers that
memorable winter of 1905 and 1906 that it will never be forgotten by
any of the unfortunate number that passed those dreary months at
Herschel Island.

The captain also told of a skilled Native crew member who offered to leave the ship with his wife and subsist by hunting rather than tax the ship's limited food supply. He was drowned, presumably while polar bear hunting, and, wrote Cook, "sadness reigned among us all, to think that one who had been so good and of so much value to us all should die in such a manner—another illustration of the self-sacrifice these natives will make for those among them who are in need of help."

Cook's boat-steerer Peterson may have been exceptional, but, according to the famous polar explorer Roald Amundsen, "whaling crews passed the time on skis in the hills." Some of their Brooks Range trips were desperate attempts by deserters to get to Yukon settlements. Many of them were recaptured, often badly frozen. A number died in the bitter, stormy cold. At least one was shot while trying to fight off pursuit. Some did make it to settlements, destitute, through what they described as "waste and mountains."

(The Firth seems to have been a well-known route. Amundsen traveled it in 1905 to give out the news that he had discovered, at last, the Northwest Passage. He noted that "Eskimos constantly travel the route and had stripped the woods." In 1918, it was probably the route used to get the seriously ill anthropologist Vilhjalmur Stefansson from Herschel Island to the Fort Yukon hospital. A good way when frozen, the Firth is a tough route in summer, when its canyon is white with rapids. The first Caucasian of record to travel the Firth, J. H. Turner of the U.S.–Canada Boundary Survey, did so in 1890, having started his trip on the Porcupine. Four years afterward, a special agent of the department of agriculture, Frederick Funston, later a general of the U.S. Army, sledded up the Sheenjek and down the Kongakut to Herschel Island and back as an adventure following his gathering of botanical specimens in the Yukon Valley.)

To get help to the whalers, men of the Royal Canadian Northwest Mounted Police mushed across the Brooks Range to the Arctic coast. One particularly respected and appreciated Mountie, a Sergeant Fitzgerald, took leave and made a special mail run in the spring of 1906 when he heard of the whalers' plight. Two years later, in the Knorr Range, Yukon Territory, he died during another such trip. He was found on the most dangerous part of the route, a barren divide, with a note beneath his head. "This is the twenty-seventh day of the blizzard," it read. "Our supplies all exhausted long ago. We have eaten our dogs, my two companions are dead, and I am dying."

During the winter and spring of 1898, in the west, a far more elaborate and ambitious traverse of the Arctic had brought relief for the crews of eight ice-bound and ice-crushed whaling vessels: food in the form of a herd of some four hundred reindeer driven seven hundred miles from the Seward Peninsula to Point Barrow.

Reindeer had been brought to Alaska as an aid to the Native economy. The experiment eventually failed. The Natives were not adept herders, and the reindeer mingled with and were absorbed by the wild caribou. For a time, however, they promised much, and they fed the desperate whalers.

Under the command of Captain Francis Tuttle of the U.S. Revenue Cutter *Bear*, the reindeer-supplying expedition gained the expert help of W. T. Kopp of the American Missionary Association, who had charge of a reindeer station at Teller. With Kopp and Native assistants in charge of the reindeer and with other sled parties also on the move, First Lieutenant D. H. Jarvis of the Revenue-Cutter Service (earlier called the Revenue Marine) led the overland trek. He left Cape Prince of Wales on February 3 with the reindeer and eighteen sleds, and arrived at Barrow on March 29. He had considered a route up the Noatak and through the De Long Mountains to the Utukok, but, as he reported, "the considerations of timber, deep snow, and the possibilities of getting lost or stalled in the mountains were too great and too much fraught with danger." Instead, the expedition generally followed the coast, but cut across the Lisburne Peninsula at the western end of the Brooks Range. On the way, Jarvis met one of the desperate whalers, George F. Tilton, mushing southward for help. Another whaling officer named Walker was making a similar perilous run via the Mackenzie River. Both hardy men survived and eventually got back to San Francisco.

B y the 1880s, a few prospectors had begun to come into the country. One of them, John Bremner, had joined Allen during his Copper River exploration. Bremner, who had a fatal misunderstanding with a Koyukon in 1891, left his name on the John River.

Bremner and others with him are credited with first finding "color" at Tramway Bar on the Middle Fork of the Koyukuk in 1887. The first gold in paying quantities was obtained there in 1893, and in 1898 the overflow of fortune hunters in the great Klondike gold rush spilled northward against the central Brooks Range. Prospectors staked hundreds of claims in the drainages of the Middle and South forks of the Koyukuk and on the Alatna. An early winter trapped nine hundred gold-seekers when the sixty-eight steamers on which they had arrived became frozen in the Koyukuk ice. Realizing that they would be trapped for a year in inhospitable country, 550 of them mushed out. The remaining 350 spent a horrible winter in rude settlements to which they gave names like Rapid City, Union City, and Jimtown. The settlement of Arctic City vainly sent the small glitter of electric lights into the arctic dark. Because of the supplies on the steamers, plus those which trader Gordon Bettles had prudently laid in, all but four of the gold-seekers survived, though they ran up $100,000 in trading-post bills. When spring came at last, the survivors pulled out, leaving behind for the Koyukuk's creeks the names of wives and sweethearts. Few had come mentally, physically, or financially equipped for the patient labor required to wrench a meager living from a harsh, remote land where the geology-dependent economy was marginal.

Nevertheless, that same year more than a thousand prospectors surged to the Kobuk on the rumor of gold, and, for a time, twelve steamers plied the river. The rush had been induced by a "conspiracy on the part of a few so-called marine transportation companies" when a spurious circular published in San Francisco told of a Kobuk strike. In a book entitled *The Truth about Alaska: The Golden Land of the Midnight Sun*, published in 1901, Eugene McElwaine of Bradford, Pennsylvania, tells the story poignantly. He was there, one of 1,254 innocents who, in the summer of 1898, landed on the beach at Cape Blossom in Kotzebue Sound. McElwaine described decent men and women of honest character who,

> *in the excitement of the hour and enchanted by the wonderful stories told of the marvelously rich finds on the Kowak [Kobuk] River, quit the staid pursuits of ordinary life and rushed into the wild and unexplored region of the Arctic to hunt for gold.*
>
> *Arriving on the ground, they speedily saw the golden fruit of promise turn to ashes in their grasp. They had been deceived.*

McElwaine estimated that about four hundred men and half a dozen women returned to the Lower Forty-Eight before winter. The rest, knowing they had been defrauded, nevertheless elected to stay, convincing themselves that in this unprospected country some lucky person might indeed find gold. McElwaine hoped that his book would serve as a warning to others who might be lured to bitter destiny:

It ought not, however, to be a sufficient indictment of the
imposters parading in the garb of respectability, who, having special
means of information, by misrepresentations and falsehoods preyed
upon the credulity of those who had none, induced a long and pitiless
journey on the part of the latter, sent many of them to their graves, and
reduced many others to a condition of lifelong debility and suffering.
More than a hundred lives were lost. Three vessels en route to the place
were sunk at sea. Five men were drowned in the sound, and sixteen on
the river. Suicides, deaths from hardship and exposure, and deaths from
freezing, occurring during the winter, went to swell the list of casualties.
About one half of the remainder had scurvy, a hideous disease. Other
ailments were, of course, contracted, incident to the change in manner
of living, to a more rigorous climate, and to the solitary existence
entailed. The scene in the spring forbids description.

A few goldseekers in the Kobuk rush got as far as the upper Noatak, and one party later went via the Noatak and Alatna to the Killik. A little gold was found in the Cosmos Hills, and placer mining also developed later in the Squirrel River Basin farther west.

A second, hardier breed of men replaced the first wave of fortune seekers in the Koyukuk country; indeed, the first three years of the twentieth century saw a major stampede to the area. During the summer of 1900, a party of prospectors went up the Dietrich River and crossed the Arctic Divide, becoming the first Caucasians to traverse the future route of the Trans-Alaska Oil Pipeline. In 1905, exaggerated rumors sent a rush briefly up the John. Still, there were enough greenhorns who got cold feet and departed that the mining center on the Middle Fork of the Koyukuk was dubbed Coldfoot.

A major buildup in productive mining of creeks tributary to the Middle Fork occurred from 1908 to 1916, with some four hundred people involved. Placer miners washed out more than $1 million worth of gold, more than all other finds, from the valleys of Nolan Creek and Hammond River. The settlement of Wiseman, upriver from Coldfoot and named for an itinerant prospector, became their base. Their Brooks Range adventures, besides prodigiously hard work, included the exploration of as much as sixty tons of bottled booze per year, as well as the attractions of as many as fourteen full-time prostitutes.

As prospectors probed the Koyukuk country, others were acquainting themselves with the eastern mountains of the Brooks. In 1901, S. J. Marsh explored the Canning, its Marsh Fork now named for him. He met and wintered in the mountains with two companions, F. G. Carter and Ned Arey, and Carter and Marsh went over to the Chandalar. There, in 1906, their gold prospects triggered a brief stampede to the only region of lode mining, all the others being placers. Arey seems to have been the first Caucasian to go into the Canning, Hulahula, Okpilak, and Jago valleys. He may well have been one of the first human beings of any race to enter the valley of the Jago, for Inupiat of the time feared it as demon-haunted.

Eventually, failing gold deposits, high wages of World War I, and prohibition drained the country of most of its miners. With the exception of a few promotional schemes and efforts to mechanize, placer mining along the southern flanks of the Brooks Range settled into a pattern of small operators content with modest rewards. Only recently has such technology as mining with scuba gear, vacuum pumps, and other innovations brought more than token productivity. Yet, as individual prospectors probed the mountains amid various boomlets and disappointments, they became steeped in their environment. Their most valued paydirt became a way of life—hard and lonely, but staunchly cherished in a country quietly appreciated.

In 1898, the federal government began systematic topographic and geologic surveys in Alaska, and geologists, joined by a few other scientists and some prospectors, assumed the responsibility of exploration in the Brooks Range. Alfred Hulse Brooks, who headed the Alaskan branch of the United States Geological Survey (USGS), called this work "far more important than any previously done, because it included both accurate topographic surveys and systematic geologic observations." "In fact," he added, "the reports based on these explorations furnished the first clue to the geography and geology of the part of Alaska north of the Yukon Basin."

For starters, in 1899, F. C. Schrader and T. G. Gerdine of the Survey, with a party of four, hauled canoes up the Chandalar River, portaged fifteen miles to the Bettles River watershed, and floated the Middle Fork of the Koyukuk, with side trips up the Dietrich River for twenty miles and also down the South Fork of the Koyukuk. In 1901, Schrader, W. J. Peters of the USGS, and six others crossed the Arctic Divide. They "milked the brush" up the John River, pulling themselves through the June freshet by grabbing riverbank vegetation. They portaged across Anaktuvuk Pass, ran the Anaktuvuk and Colville rivers, and then canoed along the coast to Point Barrow. Meanwhile, Walter C. Mendenhall, D. L. Raeburn, and a party of five were surveying the Alatna and Kobuk, portaging their canoes over the long-used Koyukon–Inupiat route from Helpmejack Creek to the upper Kobuk, and down to Kotzebue Sound.

After an eight-year hiatus in which the Geological Survey was engaged elsewhere in Alaska, the northern investigations were resumed by Philip S. Smith, and A. G. Maddren also carried geologic surveys to the Arctic Ocean in cooperation with an International Boundary Survey.

With topographer H. M. Eakin, two camp hands, and a six-horse pack train, Smith in 1910 crossed from the Koyukuk and went down the Kobuk. The following year, he and topographer C. E. Giffin, aided by four camp hands, canoed up the Alatna, portaged over to the Noatak via Portage Pass, and became the first government expedition to float what is practically the entire navigable part of the Noatak. Smith, the scientist, had praise for McLenegan, the young Revenue Marine engineer who first explored the river under dreadful conditions in the summer of 1885, although Smith wished that McLenegan had obtained "more data." Smith had less kind things to say about the work Cantwell and Stoney had done at approximately the same time, calling Cantwell's delineation of the Kobuk "unrecognizable." He commented that "the text as a whole is better than the map, but its use is in large measure dependent on personal familiarity with the region."

During the years 1906–1914, the private explorer-geologist Ernest de Koven Leffingwell was almost single-handedly making one of the most remarkable gatherings of arctic information in Alaskan history. After receiving degrees from Trinity College in Hartford, Connecticut, and undertaking graduate studies in geology and physics at the University of Chicago, Leffingwell first went north in 1901 as a geologist for the Baldwin Ziegler polar expedition. In 1906, at the age of thirty-one, he went north again with Captain Ejnar Mikkelsen, the two being joint commanders of a small expedition sponsored in part by the Royal Geographical Society and the American Geographical Society. The purpose of the expedition was to explore the Beaufort Sea with hopes of finding land north of Alaska. After wintering at Flaxman Island, they found their ship unseaworthy for the exploration, and Mikkelsen and the crew went home. Leffingwell stayed.

In all, he spent nine summers and six winters in the Arctic, making thirty-one trips by sled and boat and covering some 4,500 miles. Accompanied at times by an Inupiat or two, but often alone, he lived in a tent during much of the thirty months of his expeditions. Leffingwell's report tells of storms that pinned him in camp, of winds that blew his instruments awry, and overflows that froze them and ruined his mapping paper after his many miles of arduous travel. Yet he made the first accurate chart of the coastline between Point Barrow and Demarcation Bay, explored the Okpilak, Hulahula, Sadlerochit, and Canning rivers, and identified the Sadlerochit sandstone formation later found to be the main reservoir of Prudhoe Bay oil. Indeed, he noted reports of oil seepage and the possibility of an Arctic Slope oil field.

Leffingwell was the first scientist to make a close study of ground ice (what today is known as permafrost).

He contributed his findings to the U.S. Geological Survey as its Professional Paper 109, published in 1919. Entitled "The Canning River Region, Northern Alaska," it covers not only detailed geography, geology, and permafrost, but also such information as arctic equipment, an explanation of how he did his mapping, and the history of arctic exploration in the region and its place names.

Alfred Brooks paid this tribute in the preface to Leffingwell's report on a region of arctic Alaska that was almost unknown:

> *Mr. Leffingwell has performed a most valuable service in mapping its geography and geology. However, as this report will show, his researches were by no means limited to these subjects, for he has recorded facts and made interpretations relating to many problems in other fields of science.*
>
> *The field was one of his own choice, and the explorations were made at his own initiative and expense. Therefore the results here set forth are in every sense of the word entirely Mr. Leffingwell's own contribution to science and to a better understanding of Arctic Alaska.*
>
> *The modest narrative of his explorations here presented gives but a very inadequate conception of the self-sacrifice and hardships he endured during the years of his exploration. The reader of this volume should, however, constantly bear in mind the very adverse conditions under which the field work was done.*

Like Henry Allen, Leffingwell is an unsung hero of Alaskan exploration. Had he not gone into a completely different career after his arctic experience—fruit and nut horticulture in California—he might have become a major figure in Alaskan history.

So might Rudolph Martin Anderson, for many years chief of the division of biology of the National Museum of Canada. Anderson went to the Arctic in 1908 with Vilhjalmur Stefansson on an anthropological expedition sponsored by the American Museum of Natural History. During the four ensuing years, Stefansson left Anderson on his own for much of the time, and the biologist often lived with the Inupiat and on the resources of the country. Leffingwell credits him with being the first Caucasian to cross the Arctic Divide between the Hulahula and the Chandalar drainages. Later, Anderson was Stefansson's second-in-command on the famous explorer's Canadian Arctic Expedition of 1913, but the two men, who had been friends since college, developed deep disagreements.

Reserved, diffident, though of great physical strength and endurance, Anderson was "never more happy than when he was sitting at the door of a tent, legs outstretched, skinning a mixed bag of shrews, marmots, sandpipers, and perhaps one or two eiders, the while keeping both ears attuned to the murmur of wind and water, and the twittering of birds." So wrote a companion, anthropologist Diamond Jenness, in a 1961 obituary. "Indians and Eskimos alike trusted and admired him, because he shared so fully their own love of nature and its wild life," Jenness added. "I like best to remember him as the indefatigable traveler, cheerfully marching through the snow at the head of his weary dog-team in the waning twilight of an arctic day." Anderson reportedly had a keen sense of humor. In a *Catalogue of Canadian Recent Mammals,* he included *Homo sapiens,* and defined the European subspecies as having "dispositions aggressive and tendencies destructive."

In 1923, President Warren Harding set aside a huge chunk of the Arctic Slope as a Naval Petroleum Reserve (now called the National Petroleum Reserve in Alaska), stretching from the Arctic Divide to the sea. Knowledge of its resources was needed, and the Geological Survey mounted what was to be a series of expeditions remarkable in many ways for their daring and hardship. To study such a remote area, the geologists knew that they had to make every day count, so they mushed into the country with dogteams hauling canoes, and floated out as fall freezeup neared.

In 1924, an expedition led by Philip Smith sledded up the Alatna and Unakserak valleys and, when spring came, canoed down the Killik to the Colville. For the canoeing, the party divided, Smith leading one group, John B. Mertie, Jr., the other. Smith's party in two cedar freight canoes explored the upper Colville, Etivluk, and Awuna, and then went down the Ikpikpuk, mistaking it for the Meade. Mertie's two-canoe team went down the Colville and Ikpikpuk after exploring the Okokmilaga River, which they thought was the Chandler.

As the Mertie party waded across flooded icefields, sharp ice punched holes in the bottoms of their canoes. They dodged bergs or bottom ice as big as houses. They lined the Killik's rapids, wading the icy waters, then tried to run a stretch. Mertie's canoe was engulfed. When they reached the Colville, Mertie, despite an injured, swollen foot, made a three-day, eighty-five-mile search to find a route to the Ikpikpuk, a shallow creek up which they dragged their heavy-laden canoes for thirty miles with the water level falling. The creek forked, the riffles became almost dry, and the party had to shovel out a channel. "Maybe we would make it to the Ikpikpuk drainage and maybe not," Mertie recounted, so they called their goal Maybe Creek.

"I pulled and dragged until I saw stars," Mertie recalled, "yet by ten hours of continuous labor and extreme drudgery, we made only four miles air-line. To make matters worse, the mosquitoes were now in full blast." Unable to feed their dogteams, they had had to shoot them. The one remaining dog, Prince, was so tortured by mosquitoes that he, too, had to be put out of his misery. They buried him beside a stream and named it Prince Creek in his honor.

After seven grueling days, they started the equally difficult eight-mile portage, dragging the canoes empty across the tussocks, and packing the gear in seventy-pound loads. It was an eight-day job, and the destination creek—the portage end—was dry! "We would be all summer getting down to flowing water," lamented Mertie. "Never had I looked for rain as I did then." It came.

While Smith and Mertie were working the Colville–Ikpikpuk region, William T. Foran and O. L. Wix made an even more arduous journey farther west. Their party of five, using two canoes, went up the Kuk and Kaolak to the Utukok and Colville drainages; then, after caching one canoe and a ton of supplies and equipment, packed across the De Long Mountains from Noluk Lake to the headwaters of the Nimiuktuk, a tributary of the Noatak. "The weather was so cold, and fire wood so scarce, that water in kettle would freeze before it could get warm enough to combat temperature. Fire would die down before heat was effective. May have to use tent poles and personal effects to make fire for cooking," Foran wrote in his notebook. Moreover, so dry and so late was the season that the half-starved group found no boatable water until they came to within six miles of the Noatak.

As the five weakened men ran the swift, shallow Noatak in one leaky canoe with but four inches of freeboard, Foran shot a seagull—a lifesaver that tasted like chicken, he noted. It nearly became a death causer, however, for when the famished men devoured it, one accused another of stealing and gulping down the seagull's gizzard, which was apparently missing when every morsel counted. Foran secured the gun to avert possible murder, but the quarrel smoldered on until the group reached Kotzebue. There a trader explained that seagulls, being scavengers, have no gizzards, and friendship was reestablished. (The trader was wrong; a seagull does, in fact, have a gizzard, but it is very small.)

In reporting on the Foran–Wix exploration, Smith noted that it

necessitated an almost continuous portage of about 60 miles, in which three divides were crossed, one of them about 4,000 feet above sea level, in the short time between August 5 and September 16, and was an achievement that could have been carried through only by the indefatigable efforts of every member of the party and by the resourcefulness and indomitable pluck and generalship of Foran, the leader.

Throughout all that travail they carried an outboard motor.

In 1925, Gerald Fitzgerald, who had been with Smith and Mertie in 1924, led another grand circuit up the Noatak and Kugururak to the Utukok and Colville by sled, down the Colville and up the Etivluk by canoe, using dog power and shoveling to get through, and down the Aniuk to the Noatak again. Smith led a more westerly trip in 1926 from Kivalina to the Kokolik, dodging crashing snowdrifts fifty feet high and 100 yards long.

These Brooks Range traversals to explore the remote geology of the petroleum reserve were among the last of the great treks done in the old, tough manner of mushing, canoeing, and backpacking without the aid of aircraft. I say "among" because another breed of scientist was beginning to join the geologists in the wilderness: the wildlife biologist. Rudolph Anderson was one. Two others of note were the Murie brothers, Olaus and Adolph, who mushed up the Alatna and Kutuk in the winter of 1922–1923 on a caribou survey. With his wife, Margaret, Olaus was later to make trips up the Old Crow and Sheenjek rivers—trips that helped confirm the Muries' leadership in establishing the Arctic National Wildlife Refuge.

To us latecomers whose wilderness exercise was taken after a quick fly-in by airplane or helicopter, the exploits of the scientist-explorers seemed truly heroic. They continued, of course, with increasingly mechanical assistance from tracked vehicles and aircraft. But the geology profession's characteristic thoroughness and endurance has sent men like Bill Brosge, Bob Chapman, Bob Coates, Bob Detterman, Tom Dutro, Art and Mick Lachinbruch, Bill Patton, Hill Reiser, Ed Sable, Irv Tailleur, and others tramping the ridges, running the rivers as before. On one expedition in 1945, it took George Gryc, Carl Steffanson, and Ed Webber thirty days to pack boats and gear thirty miles down the flooded Chandler River. Marv Mangus carried a pedometer and logged 1,200 miles one summer, 2,100 another. Caches would be placed in April by vehicle or plane, and the geologists would map their way from one to the next.

The year 1955 saw the last of the boat parties, and after 1957, helicopters became key aids to geological exploration and mapping. For more than a decade, the 'copters were used mainly to move camps, however. The field work was still done mostly afoot. The geologists would cover ten to forty miles a day, carrying rock samples. Now, the helicopters flit like bees from summit to summit. If marked on a map, their landing places would fairly pepper the vast region through which Philip Smith trekked in 1911 and 1924. By 1976, a year after I had hiked to a ridge that perhaps no non-Native had reached before, that same ridge had become just another routine helicopter checkpoint. Yet geology continues to be a boot-sole profession, as latter-day leaders in Alaskan geology like Don Grybeck and Gil Mull can testify. Thomas D. Hamilton, a glacial geologist who accompanied me on a Wild River study of the Noatak, thought nothing of walking six or seven miles each evening after a long day's paddling.

I have heard no better expression of admiration for the work of the U.S. Geological Survey than that of George Collins, the National Park Service planner who received Survey encouragement and much assistance in his studies of what was to become the Arctic National Wildlife Refuge: "I don't think that the public generally realizes how much the geologist is an explorer, a great explorer, one who defines into factual knowledge, insofar as that's possible in any field, the rumors and hunches and the ideas that are prevalent, almost like romance stories that could hardly be credible otherwise." The Survey, Collins remarked, is "replete with brilliant minds—fine people, excellent outdoorsmen. Some of the best woodsmen in the world are geologists of the USGS. They do fantastic things that you never hear of, in terms of climbing around out in the mountains."

The USGS men are wont to understate their accomplishments, but their indomitable spirit is legendary. W. C. Mendenhall remarked that "observations made while the observer is struggling ahead at the end of a tracking line, or bending all his energies to the prevention of disaster in the wild waters of a gorge, or perhaps zigzagging up a thousand-foot climb with ninety pounds on his back, are not always as complete as is desirable." In truth, as National Park Service historian Bill Brown has noted, they made exquisite maps and drawings, though their notebooks were blurred with sweat and blood.

Geologists no longer have to make their own basic maps as they go. The Brooks Range is all mapped now. There are no more blank spaces. The 30th Engineers Battalion of the Army Map Service saw to that after World War II. The geology of much of the range was really not comprehended until the 1950s, however, and geologists say there are still little-known areas, still secrets to discover, or discover again. Though the ranges be gaunt and open, something may be hidden among them. In 1958, the Brooks Range swallowed up Clarence Rhode, the Alaska director of the U.S. Fish and Wildlife Service. The biggest aerial search in Alaska up to that time ensued, but the wreckage of his airplane was not found for twenty-one years.

Bob Marshall embraces two of his companions, Jesse Allen (left) and Nutirwik (right), on the last of his Brooks Range expeditions. (Courtesy The Bancroft Library, University of California, Berkeley)

THEN
CAME
BOB MARSHALL

Life's most splendid moments come in the opportunity to enjoy undefiled nature.

—Robert Marshall

By the late 1920s, military men, geologists, and biologists had explored up and down most of the major drainages of the Brooks Range, and had crested many of its principal passes. Most of the river approaches to the range had been mapped, at least partially, as had the huge petroleum reserve on the Arctic Slope.

A large blank spot remained on the maps, however, centered in the drainage of the North Fork of the Koyukuk River. A few trappers and prospectors had probed the country, for their principal northern settlement, Wiseman, was on the Koyukuk's Middle Fork nearby, but there had been no methodical map-making explorations. Thank goodness for that remaining blank spot, for it attracted Robert Marshall.

Bob Marshall is to the Brooks Range what Henry Thoreau is to the Maine woods and John Muir to the Sierra Nevada. Marshall's appreciation, imbued with vigor, infectious enthusiasm, and eloquence, became the root of the conservation movement to perpetuate an arctic wilderness in Alaska.

The Adirondack summers of his youth instilled in Marshall a love of the outdoors and made him an indefatigable hiker. After earning a master's degree in forestry and a doctorate in plant physiology, he joined the U.S. Forest Service, and later became director of forestry for the Office of Indian Affairs. Not long before a heart attack in 1939 took his life in its prime, he rejoined the Forest Service as chief of the Division of Lands and Recreation. Like his contemporary in conservation, forester/ecologist Aldo Leopold, Marshall recognized the value of wilderness both

69

to science and to human recreation. Disturbed by the many forces that were shrinking the roadless areas of the United States, he led in the establishment of a system of wilderness designations in national forests and on Indian reservations. Along with Leopold, Marshall was among the founders of The Wilderness Society, which led the long struggle for an act to protect American wilderness areas permanently by law. The Wilderness Act finally came to pass in 1964.

Longing for the adventure of true exploration, Marshall, then twenty-eight, took some vacation time in 1929 to head for the least-known part of Alaska. His professional excuse was to study arctic tree growth, but the real allure was those unmapped spaces that had so fascinated him since boyhood. It was the first of four trips he made to the central Brooks Range. Those travels and sojourns yielded not only a best-selling book of 1933, *Arctic Village,* about the community of Wiseman, where he lived for almost a year, but also included hundreds of summer and winter days of wilderness adventuring with trapper-prospector friends. He explored not only the North Fork of the Koyukuk and its tributaries but also parts of the Dietrich River, and upper Hammond, the John, the Alatna, and the Anaktuvuk and Killik headwaters, and made a foray up the Chandalar. He mapped some twelve thousand square miles hitherto uncharted, and climbed twenty-eight major mountain peaks. His journals and letters about those experiences, some published in periodicals, others privately circulated among friends, were collected and edited by his brother George as *Arctic Wilderness,* published in 1956. A second edition in 1970 was entitled *Alaska Wilderness.* It is a book not only for fireside dreams but also one to set in motion attic rummagings for camping equipment, establishment of savings accounts, and consultation with airlines. Scratch almost any Brooks Range wanderer these days and you will find a would-be Bob Marshall. His spirit imbues every adventure in arctic Alaska.

Marshall used a number of key words to convey what he considered to be the meaning and benefit of his experiences. Near his beloved Mount Doonerak, he wrote of being "in a constant ecstasy." He mentions humility as well, independence, discovery, solitude, and the freshness of the splendor that he found. One senses Marshall's profound spiritual reveling when he explains,

> *I yearned for adventures comparable to those of Lewis and Clark. I realized that the field for geographical exploration was giving out, but kept hoping that one day I might have the opportunity for significant geographical discovery. And now I found myself here, at the very headwaters of one of the mightiest rivers of the north, with dozens of never-visited valleys and hundreds of unscaled summits still as virgin as during their Paleozoic creation.*

I spent more than three bright hours up there on top of the continent, looking in every direction over miles of wilderness in which, aside from Lew and Al, I knew there was not another human being. This knowledge, this sense of independence which it gave, was second only to the sense of perfect beauty instilled by the scenery on all sides.

One can almost feel the adrenaline that pumped into Bob Marshall's bloodstream when "there was again the delicious feeling of exploring untrodden ground and a half spooky sensation that some supernatural phenomenon might be just ahead. . . . Supreme exaltation . . . came that moment I crossed the skyline and gazed over into the winter-buried mystery of the Arctic . . . where fact and infinity merged. . . . All was peace and strength and immensity and coordination and freedom."

In helping to organize The Wilderness Society, Marshall subscribed to the manifesto "the wilderness (and the environment of solitude) is a natural mental resource having the same basic relation to man's ultimate thought and culture as coal, timber, and other physical resources have to his material needs." He loved being far from what he called "a civilization remote from nature, artificial, dominated by the exploitation of man by man." He admitted that his attitude might seem unbelievable. "Here it was also unreal," he reflected regarding the Brooks Range, "but it was the unreality of a freshness beyond experience.

"At every step there was the exhilarating feeling of breaking new ground. There were no musty signs of human occupation, not even the psychological depression that nothing could be new. For this beyond a doubt was an unbeaten path."

Bob Marshall was no loner. He relished good companionship, and his writings glow with the good times he had among the people of Wiseman and with the partners of his wilderness travels. He echoed the feelings of many friends who have adventured together when he recalled,

We didn't say very much sitting there. You don't when it is your last camp with a companion who has shared the most perfect summer of a lifetime. We just sat, with a feeling warmer than the cracking fire, exulting in the sharp-edged pattern which the mountain walls cut against the northern sky; listening to the peaceful turmoil of the arctic river with its infinite variation in rhythm and tone; smelling the luxuriance of arctic breezes on cheeks and hair.

Nor was he a macho proclaimer of deeds of derring-do. Despite the exuberance of his accounts, there is no bragging, tough-guy, look-what-I-did spirit. "As I walked for hours beneath the stupendous grandeur . . . I felt humble and insignificant," he confessed.

For all his joyous enthusiasm, Marshall did not gloss over hazards and travails—the hard, miserable times he experienced. He rose above them, neither reveling in the mastery of them nor using the incidents to scare or overawe his readers. "On the whole the going was good," he wrote; "but the last five miles, through clumps of sedges, made a substantial installment on the required payment for our one week in heaven." His reports make clear the dangers of high water, for he was washed out of camp and later nearly drowned when a boat capsized. They also note the necessity of walking around creeks that cannot be forded, and that can mean miles and miles of sidehill trudging, fighting through alder thickets, and crossing side canyons.

Marshall was a prodigious hiker, no doubt about that. In 1932, he climbed fourteen Adirondack peaks in one "great" day, ascending a total of 13,600 feet in less than seventeen hours. He was probably not as concerned about detours as others might be. However, I cannot help but feel that in his vigor and enthusiasm he may sometimes have exaggerated his traveling speed. Having tried to keep up with U.S. Supreme Court Justice William O. Douglas's habitual four-mile-an-hour gait along a canal towpath, I find it hard to believe Marshall when he says, "We were fresh and going four miles an hour at the end of thirty trackless miles," and "covered four uphill miles in little more than an hour." Maybe so. Marshall's brother George recalls their making five miles an hour on some of the Adirondack road walks of their youth. On one they covered sixty miles in one day. The ridge-running geologists, like the Native hunters, say they can cover twenty to forty miles in a day (as compared with the six I'm used to). But the Brooks Range is a country where one can seldom take a full stride or keep a steady pace. One can usually just stumble along. Perhaps Marshall practiced a version of the hiker's dance that Keith Nyitray called the "tundra two-step." But that would have been hard for Marshall to do when, for example, he walked out to Wiseman for new supplies after a near-fatal capsize, for he had to hike in heavy rubber hip boots. He had lost his shoes, probably the rubber-bottomed, high-laced shoepacs he favored along with sneakers, and the kind used by the Muries and popular with other Brooks Range travelers today. Nevertheless, he made the seventy-five miles in three days of nine-hour-a-day hiking. Though his pack was light, his overall rate of about three miles an hour is impressive.

Marshall and his locally recruited companions—prospectors and trappers—were able to lighten their loads by living off the country to some extent, shooting a sheep or catching a few grayling for their suppers, and their other foods were simple, mostly dry items. However, they lacked not only the modern-day array of freeze-dried foods but also the advantages of nylon and other strong, warm but featherweight materials. I have no doubt that today Marshall would revel in such efficient, gentle-on-the-land equipment.

Having come into the country with the use of horses, a motorboat, or dogsled, he often hiked out of base camps traveling light. However, he also shouldered loads "reduced to 65 pounds" or more, and these were not modern frame packs that fit and distribute weight so well. Judging from photographs and his mention of headstraps, it would seem that he was using a pack he had designed for his trips in the Adirondacks, similar to what I would call a "Maine guide's pack": a great bulbous sack with a tumpline attached as well as shoulder straps. Such capacious instruments of torture were designed for portages, but I have carried one in the Sierra Nevada, and I shall spend a considerable time in purgatory for the resultant swearing.

In his excitement and enthusiasm, Marshall somewhat exaggerated his descriptions of the scenery. He called areas "grander than Yosemite" when they are really not. There are no domes beside which Yosemite's Half Dome "would be trivial." This was not deliberate, I am convinced, for Marshall was no Baron Münchausen or Arkansas tale-spinner. His was the exaggeration born of first-on-the-scene appreciative and awed excitement. He himself acknowledged the pointlessness of comparisons, anyway: "Every one of the mountains had innumerable precipices, a thousand, two thousand, even three thousand feet high. It did not really matter—there were no measures in this world—and after seeing the superlative so long, space began to lose its significance."

Marshall's descriptions were nonetheless valid if somewhat overstated. One of the most beautiful in wilderness literature, I think, is his description of Loon Lake. From it one can infer how greatly his aesthetic judgments were conditioned by his thrill of discovery. "No sight or sound or smell or feeling even remotely hinted of men or their creations," he wrote. "It seemed as if time had dropped away a million years and we were back in a primordial world. It was like discovering an unpeopled universe where only the laws of nature held sway."

Marshall expressed great excitement at seeing the Arrigetch upthrust of granite. Calling them "sensational, needlelike peaks," he reported the Inupiat name meaning Fingers of the Hand Extended and commented that it "admirably expresses the appearance of these mountains." From a parallel ridge, Marshall and his companion, the redoubtable trapper-prospector Ernie Johnson, took a good look at what is among the most astounding sights among mountains anywhere and photographed them, but he burst into no ecstatic descriptive paean as he so often did for the Koyukuk's North Fork country. I can only conclude that he did not relate as well to mountains he despaired of ascending, for he simply wrote, "Since neither Ernie nor I belonged to the human-fly category, we did not try to climb the Arrigetch peaks."

He felt quite differently about his adored Mount Doonerak, the "Matterhorn of the Koyukuk," which he longed, and tried, to climb. Bad weather and the realization that the climb was probably a technical one, beyond his skills and equipment, caused him philosophically to give up hope for such an achievement. (The 7,457-foot summit was attained in 1952 by experienced climbers who found it surprisingly easy.)

M arshall's greatest descriptive coup was his naming of the Gates of the Arctic, that yawning two-mile-wide *U* through which the North Fork of the Koyukuk passes between mighty gateposts. Marshall named them Boreal Mountain and Frigid Crags.

"The mountains became more and more precipitous until finally they culminated in the Gates of the Arctic," he wrote. "Here on the west side of the valley a whole set of bristling crags, probably at least a score, towered sheer for perhaps 2,000 feet from an exceedingly steep 2,000-foot pedestal. From a similar base on the east rose the 4,000-foot precipice of Boreal." In view of his frequent overstatement of grandeur, it is surprising to learn from his notebooks that Marshall apparently first *underestimated* the heights here.

There are a number of formations in the Brooks Range that resemble in shape, size, and significance the Koyukuk Gates, but so evocative has been the name that it has captured the imagination of all who have heard it. It did much to bring about national park status for the area. When it was first proposed that the area become part of the National Park System, the Park Service suggested to Secretary of the Interior Stewart Udall a two-unit national monument for outgoing President Lyndon Johnson to proclaim. An east unit included the Gates; a west one, the Arrigetch Peaks, Walker Lake, the upper Kobuk River, and Mount Igikpak. The Bureau of Land Management (which then administered the area and thought that it might have mineral potential) at first talked the secretary out of the east unit. When Udall learned that he would lose the name along with the unit, however, he changed his mind. Apparently, the name failed to move the president as it did the secretary and so many others. Johnson did not sign the proclamation.

The Arrigetch Peaks, Gates of the Arctic National Preserve. (National Park Service photograph by Robert Belous)

Even as he camped amid the Gates of the Arctic, viewing a pristine world hundreds of miles from the nearest automobile, Bob Marshall sensed its susceptibility to exploitation. Had it been more conveniently located, it would long since have been roaded and developed in ways that would clash with its wild sublimity.

During the park studies of the region in the early 1970s, my companions and I used to chuckle at a sick joke of ours that imagined a huge hotel arisen in the Gates. It was complete, we fancied, with an Ernie Johnson Cocktail Lounge and a Bob Marshall Ballroom. A small beginning of such a perverse fantasy actually took form as a semipermanent guides' camp, where hikers and boaters could obtain a bit of the salving of civilization. It took the Park Service years to muster the courage to get rid of it.

Even as he ranged through its vastness, Bob Marshall realized the limited ability of the country to sustain uses like his own for large numbers of people. I feel certain that had he walked up Arrigetch Creek, seen the attractiveness of that spectacular area and the narrow, dead-end approach, he would have immediately sensed its severe limitations and vulnerability. "If the millions wanted this sort of perfection and could attain it," he observed, "the values of freshness and remoteness and adventure beyond the paths of men would automatically disappear."

> *Actually, only a small minority of the human race will ever consider primeval nature a basic source of happiness. For this minority, tracts of wilderness paradise urgently need preservation. But mankind as a whole is too numerous for its problem of happiness to be solved by the simple expedient of paradise, whether it lies in Eden or the flower-filled Amawk divide.*

In the introduction to the first edition of his brother's book, *Arctic Wilderness,* George Marshall quotes some of Bob's other writings that confirm his assessment of the worth of wilderness, of the Brooks Range as a treasury of it, and his hopes that it be kept so for the future. Bob Marshall knew that wilderness, like great art or music, is a delectation for a minority but, because of its importance to the human mind and spirit, must be available to all. "There is a point," he once argued, "where an increase in the joy of the many causes a decrease in the joy of the few out of all proportion to the gain of the former."

"In wilderness, with its entire freedom from the manifestations of human will, that perfect objectivity which is essential for pure aesthetic rapture can probably be achieved more readily than among any other forms of beauty," Marshall wrote.

"The unexplored areas of the world are becoming distinctly limited. Consequently, since they are capable of giving such superb value to human beings, it is desirable that the possibility of exploration be prolonged as much as possible."

Marshall decried "mechanical ingenuity" as destructive to the "value of isolation" in the wilderness. He himself esteemed "pitting oneself without the aid of machinery against unknown Nature," and commented: "When you use machinery to get the jump on Nature by making her reveal some of her secrets in advance, it seems to me a little bit like peeping at the end of a book to see how the plot will come out." Extolling the physical and mental challenges of wilderness adventure, he declared that "life without such exertions would be for many persons a dreary game, scarcely bearable in its horrible banality."

On the basis of his intense Brooks Range experiences, and as a champion for wilderness, Marshall pronounced that "when Alaska recreation is viewed from a national standpoint, it becomes at once obvious that its highest value lies in the pioneer conditions yet prevailing throughout most of the territory.... In Alaska alone can the emotional values of the frontier be preserved." In those pre-statehood, pre-oil days, he recommended that most of Alaska north of the Yukon River be closed to road building and industrial development: "Alaska is unique among all recreational areas belonging to the United States because Alaska is yet largely a wilderness. In the name of a balanced use of American resources, let's keep northern Alaska largely a wilderness."

Walker Lake, first a National Landmark and now a central jewel of the Gates of the Arctic National Park. (National Park Service photograph by M. Woodbridge Williams)

RANGE
WRITINGS

When you're with nature, flowing with the power of the earth, that's when you burst forth as a person.

—Christian P. B. Johnson

*A*rctic Village, Robert Marshall's sociological account of his sojourn in the waning gold town of Wiseman, was, except for Geological Survey reports, the first publication treating a northern Alaskan area since a few turn-of-the-century descriptions of the gold rush.

Other experiential literature began to flower about a dozen years later when, in the mid-1940s, Harmon ("Bud") and Constance Helmericks saw opportunity in the Alatna Valley. The enterprising young army veteran and his wife canoed up the river and wintered there, returning later by airplane after Bud capitalized on his army flight training to become an Alaskan bush pilot. The couple used their experiences as grist for lectures and for five books, two dealing particularly with the Alatna area and their life of hunting and trapping: *We Live in the Arctic* (1947) and *The Flight of the Arctic Tern* (1952). Written from Connie Helmericks's perspective, these were the first popular accounts to present a detailed and absorbing picture of wilderness life and survival, wherein one grizzly bear meant more in food value than all the provisions they had hauled upriver.

Although imbued with the adventuresome spirit of a pioneering lifestyle (including some fine praise for hunting as an appropriate enterprise for women), the Helmerickses' books seemed to mark a turning point from an older exploitative, derring-do approach to a more appreciative view of wilderness. Hunting, though necessary and enjoyed, is recounted with respect for the prey. The Helmerickses speak of the rights of bears, and say that cutting down four-hundred-year-old trees gave them an "odd feeling as though doing wrong." The writing has many eloquent passages about the "glowing land." It also expresses some deep, early-on concerns about that land's ability to sustain ever-increasing hunting pressure by people subsisting on arctic wildlife in an area where a hunter needs a hundred square miles of territory.

The Helmerickses joined in Marshall's eloquent call for wilderness protection in the north. "Only here is there left in North America an area which is like it originally was, where a person can observe the past in the present and possibly predict the future," they wrote, observing the impact of their minor trail construction. "Why try to make Alaska what it was never meant to be? Why destroy our wilderness resources: the only important crop which Alaska is now producing or is likely soon to produce."

They reveled in the inaccessibility of the Brooks Range, yet they "never had any doubt from the beginning that the arctic world would, or at least should, become a world playground in time: its vacation possibilities are stupendous." This thought apparently grew in Bud Helmericks's mind into what later appeared to be ambivalence toward the wilderness he had extolled. Divorced from Constance and having become a noted big-game guide, he began to capitalize on his Brooks Range land claims on Walker Lake. "Any person could have that lake just for settling there," he and Constance had written, and he did in fact claim and build upon three sites on that jewel of the Brooks Range wilderness. One building was a modern three-story dwelling right on the shore, first planned as a teaching center but later becoming a commercial lodge.

But back in 1952, he and Constance worried about the "world playground" scenario: "There was always that strong antisocial intuition, that inner voice which tells every Alaskan to be cautious when he praises Alaska," Constance wrote.

" 'I have given you everything,' the voice said. 'I have nurtured you in your prodigal days. Now, even you, too, betray me.'

"The trouble is that you can't share wilderness. When you share it the wilderness is no more. . . . Wilderness given to the tender mercies of 250 million people, is doomed."

Recently, Bud Helmericks apparently heard that voice again, and remembered the twinges of conscience when doing something that might threaten wilderness values. He and his second wife, Martha, agreed to sell the lodge to the park, and the structure has been demolished. As he was considering this, he wrote me:

> *The dream we all had of a wilderness park in creating The Gates of the Arctic* [Park] *. . . have faded and we need to revive them once more. We still have a wonderful chance.*

I am so glad Martha and I saw it when it was real wilderness for
we do know what and why and how wilderness is. . . . We developed
a very good lodge on Walker Lake, but we realize that such a successful
business is the opposite of wilderness, so we have plans to go back to our
original dream. . . . There can't be a compromise with wilderness—like
faith you can't have degrees—you have it or you don't.

Constance Helmericks was the first of four women whose eloquent words about the Brooks Range offer important, detailed insights into what life in that environment can mean. To Lois Crisler, that life was in terms of the animals, and she disagreed with other wilderness advocates who have asserted that living off the country is essential to true intimacy with the wild.

She and her cinematographer husband Herb went to the Brooks on assignment from Walt Disney to film caribou, wolves, and other arctic wildlife. They spent eighteen months camped on the tundra, returning to Barrow only when the Big Dark came with its bitter cold. Rearing wolves, they watched the arctic pageant of animal life. In a foreword to Lois Crisler's 1958 book, *Arctic Wild*, A. Starker Leopold pointed out that whereas Robert Marshall's wilderness view was topographic and scenic, Crisler's was "a great living whole, with its proper animals going about their business." (Starker, a son of the famous Aldo, gained his own distinction as a professor of zoology at the University of California.)

"How a land is furnished and comforted when its animals show up in it," she exclaimed. "Great wilderness has two characteristics: remoteness and the presence of wild animals in something like pristine variety and numbers. Remoteness cannot be imitated in cheap materials; and wilderness without animals is mere scenery."

In an article written in 1957 for *The Living Wilderness* magazine, Crisler explained that

No place looks deader than the Arctic. But here in these stern
mountains a human in our own generation may see more life than the
once-rich temperate zone any longer affords. For 12 years my husband
and I lived only in the so-called wilderness areas of the United States,
but we never saw wilderness till we came to the Brooks Range. Here the
wilderness is complete—ground cover, flowers, birds, thousands of
animals big and small. It is almost the only authentic living wilderness
left for humans to learn from—to learn something more important
than scientific knowledge; to learn the feel of a full response to a total

*situation involving other lives. Learn that the esthetic response to nature
is only one note in a living response to life.*

*The wonder of the Brooks Range is the wonder of the life that
survives here. Very swiftly it can be destroyed. Then where could we
experience awe and wonder—those cleansing feelings that re-shape
and humanize our inner selves? On other planets?*

The third woman to write about the Brooks Range was Margaret E. Murie, whose popular *Two in the Far North* came out in 1963 but covers more years of Alaskan experience than the other women's books. Beginning in 1911, and based on vivid recollections and detailed diaries of travels with her wildlife biologist husband Olaus, her book glows with a woman's kind, positive vigor. With so much for her to see and do (including, on one trip, caring for their baby), the stories are too warm-hearted and active for long contemplative reflections. "Mardy" Murie's appreciative philosophy gleams forth nevertheless:

> *I know nothing of painting, but I felt for a moment the urge a
> landscape painter must experience—to brush great strokes of brown and
> fawn and purple-gray and silver upon canvas. Gazing at such a scene,
> through half-closed eyes, from a mountaintop strikes through to your
> inmost heart. The place, the scene, the breeze, the bird song, the fragrance
> of myriad brave burgeoning mosses and flowers—all blend into one
> clear entity—one jewel. It is the Arctic in its unbelievably accelerated
> summer life. It is also the personal well-being purchased by striving—
> by lifting and setting down your legs, over and over, through the muskeg,
> up the slopes, gaining the summit—man using himself. This wondrous
> mingling of weariness and triumph and sudden harmony with the
> exquisite airs, the burgeoning life of the bird and plant world of the tops,
> is part of the "glad tidings," surely, which John Muir meant when he
> said, "Climb the mountains and get their glad tidings."*

When the Muries were heading downriver toward home, she wrote: "From here on out we would be closing out of the wilderness, away from perfect solitude and unsullied country . . . we would be leaving perfect at-oneness with the untouched." Expressions like that gave *Two in the Far North* its vicarious appeal to readers longing to realize a legendary Alaska.

Mardy Murie found space in her eventful narrative for some characteristic cogency regarding wilderness use:

*We all agreed that many people could see and live in and enjoy
this wilderness in the course of a season, if they would just come a very
few at a time, never a party larger than six, and then leave the camp
site absolutely neat. It is possible, and this attitude of consideration, and
reverence, is an integral part of an attitude toward life, toward the
unspoiled, still evocative places on our planet. If man does not destroy
himself through his idolatry of the machine, he may learn one day to
step gently on his Earth.*

Looking back on her experiences in Alaska and her subsequent home, the
Tetons of Wyoming, Mardy Murie later explained in a National Park Service
interview: "I don't think once having had a great experience in wilderness you could
ever abandon wilderness in your thoughts. And at every opportunity that came your
way to preserve wilderness you would be in there fighting for it, no matter what your
other occupations might be. And in that way you'd be achieving real citizenship in
this country. That's what my hope for tomorrow is."

Olaus Murie was also a writer, although his scientific work, conservation
activism, and wildlife art may have overshadowed his literary accomplishments. His
book, *Journeys to the Far North*, published posthumously in 1976, includes some
moving and insightful philosophy. Here are some combined excerpts.

*Will we have the patience to understand what the northern part
of the Earth has to offer? Wherever we went in this country, there was
something to see and wonder about. There were so many little things.
The birds we saw, the caribou, bear, wolf, and so many other natural
manifestations gave life to the land. They inspired us to go places, to see,
to appreciate, and to try to understand. We can get the full appreciation
of all this if we enter the Arctic humbly, with an inquiring mind, and
look for the modest beauty to be found all about us.*

Some of the beauty was not so modest. "In August," Murie wrote, "autumn
paints the blueberry bushes, cranberries, dwarf birch, and all the other growth, and
the landscape takes on the colors appropriate for that season. If you watch a caribou,
or a grizzly bear, in the midst of that—what more do you want?"

In her preface to the book, Mardy Murie tells us that her scientist husband
had an overwhelming desire to transmit, to share, his *feelings* about the Arctic: "It was
an experience difficult to repeat now, but I know that he cherished the hope that the
young might still have opportunities for great adventure if only our society is wise

Olaus and Margaret Murie start out for a day's field research in the Sheenjek Valley region, 1956. (Photograph by George B. Schaller, Wildlife Conservation International, New York Zoological Society; courtesy of Dr. Schaller)

enough to keep some of the great country in both Canada and Alaska empty of development and full of life."

Another Brooks Range couple were Billie Wright and her wilderness-wise clergyman husband Sam. The Wrights were challenged by an old Inupiat woman to live in the Native way, to try to understand "that special relationship to the environment which is the basis of the Eskimos' rare and remarkable selfhood." Billie Wright's book, *Four Seasons North*, published in 1973, is a day-to-day account of a year spent subsisting beside a Brooks Range lake in a cabin she and her husband built. She reveals that that cabin became the warm heart of a great wholeness of home— the wilderness world itself—and asserts that an "instant" wilderness experience of ten or twenty lessons does not work: "One cannot grasp the eternal 'instantly'." Of visiting friends, Billie wrote: "I think they are moving back now toward what we all still carry in our genes of ten thousand years ago, unacknowledged, unrecognized but perhaps sensed. . . .

"They are beginning—just beginning—to know. Just beginning to recognize the source out of which they were created. They are showing signs of rediscovering the universe as their home."

On another lake in the Brooks, Fred and Elaine Meader committed themselves to elemental living in the wild, rooting themselves in the values of a whole Earth and Earth spirit. Regarding their way of life, Michael Parfit, in a special 1978 issue of the magazine *New Times,* made the point that "while there is wilderness set aside for the tourist, there is no provision made for the wilderness life." "Surely," he wrote, "there is a need for places where machines are banned but not habitation, where one can confront, if only for a year or two, the unshielded radiance of your own life—to plunge wholly and gasping into the wild." Fred Meader's writing complemented Parfit's:

> *Obviously, most people do not believe it is meaningful to live in a wilderness environment. Even the so-called "wilderness lovers" would have us all think of the wilderness as a museum. But if a man's relationship to the wilderness is one of "a visitor who does not remain," then his relationship is one of sentimentality rather than love, for love cannot exist without perfect intimacy.*

This is a theme that John McPhee brought out in 1976 in his best-selling *Coming into the Country,* and it endeared him and his book to Alaskans, who have pressed for cabin-building privileges in protected areas. Yet it raises the carrying-capacity dilemma of limited resources and wear-and-tear, one alluded to by the Helmerickses. Wilderness territory, seemingly vast, can support so very few that, when one trapper moves into a valley inhabited by another, both may starve. How many inhabitants, therefore, can the wilderness sustain in a meaningful way? How many four-hundred-year-old trees could be cut; how many twenty-year-old trout caught; how many caribou, moose, or grizzly bears killed for winter meat and fat? How soon might the scars heal—in time for the next incoming resident to find the land pristinely wild?

How might wildlands dwellers be selected? In *Coming into the Country—* which must rank in the very top echelons of Alaskan literature and indeed in all of what McPhee calls "the literature of fact"—McPhee expresses the belief that the wilderness would do its own screening: the wimps, the faddists, the incompetents would fail and go back to civilization or die (though probably after leaving some scars on the country). Admiring the beautiful intrepidity of pioneer living, McPhee seems not to have allowed himself to recognize that, although the percentage of would-be wilderness dwellers will probably remain tiny, there are in our growing population more and more strong, capable, determined people who want to go live in the wilds and could do so successfully. Who shall continue to have that opportunity, and where? The Great Land is very large, but it is getting no larger. Even in Alaska, wilderness is not an unlimited resource.

McPhee's reference to this occurs in the eponymous Book III of his famous volume. It is Book I, "The Encircled River," however, that concerns the Brooks Range, at the Northern Tree Line.

"The Encircled River" gives a detailed and absorbing account of a wilderness journey down the wild Salmon that flows out of the Baird Mountains into the Kobuk. McPhee scans as with field glasses, focuses as with his monocular, examines as with a loupe. With words, he paints and he engraves. "The Encircled River" encompasses the elements needed to understand the Brooks Range, its people, its tundra, its fish, its bears. McPhee deals with the nature of Alaskans and Alaska, and with the background and debates of its conservation. These are just some of the notes and themes that make up a unique, melodious literary round. From it one can probably gain more understanding more quickly and more entertainingly than from any other comparable piece of writing.

Dropping toward sleep after a fourteen-mile walk that included a close encounter with a grizzly bear, McPhee reviews that first day in Salmon River country: "It was a vision of a whole land, with an animal in it. This was his country, clearly enough. To be there was to be incorporated, in however small a measure, into its substance—his country, and if you wanted to visit it you had better knock."

The Helmerickses, Crislers, Muries, and Wrights shared the experience of dwelling or working in the Brooks Range. Recreation in the north was then confined principally to hunting. By the early 1950s, however, the adventure and satisfactions of wilderness travel extolled by Bob Marshall had begun to attract backpackers and kayakers to the Anaktuvuk Pass–John Valley region. By 1959, the major peaks had been climbed. A three-hundred-mile, twenty-seven-day back-packing journey from Demarcation Bay to Arctic Village by Dr. Rune Lindgren of Johns Hopkins University, in 1962, seems to have been the first purely recreational trip of that length since Frederick Funston's winter trip in 1894. A University of Alaska graduate student, Richard Darrell Watt, made two backpacking trips in the range with companions that same year while preparing a master of science thesis on the range's recreational potential. Hunting guide Bernd Gaedeke, who later established himself in the upper Alatna country, walked from Barter Island to Arctic Village in 1965 and wrote about it in *Alaska Sportsman* magazine two years later. Sepp Weber of Anchorage began making lone kayak trips in the central Brooks Range at about that same time. Recreational cross-country skiing began about 1970.

Brooks Range literature shifted from paean to outcry as the shadows of mining and big oil and Native land claims fell across the range in the late 1960s. The writings that revered wilderness qualities and values became even more beautiful for their added urgency and poignancy.

Among the earliest and most elegantly eloquent of these expressions is that of John P. Milton, a widely traveled ecologist who was associated with the Conservation Foundation. His book, *Nameless Valleys, Shining Mountains,* came out in 1970. In its introduction, he explains, "I first came to this wild, free land not as a scientist, but simply a man who wanted to feel the pulse of wilderness. . . . Now, several scant years later, this same wild land faces brutal domestication by bulldozer and oil rig and greed. Only strength and soul and wisdom can save the Arctic."

Milton's book is based on a walk northward across the Arctic Wildlife Range, where "a man is swallowed whole in an expansive world, yet free . . . to seek, to explore, to discover himself." It is a very personal book, with a spare grace of thought and expression, introspective at times, and focusing often on intriguing details of scene and experience.

"First, I am impressed by the space, the vastness, and the far mountains lining the horizon," Milton writes of crossing the Arctic Slope. "Then my eye is caught by the subtle shadings of brown and green, the delicate forms and contours of the nearly level landscape. Lastly, a bit of green moss, a brown and white mushroom, a flower of blue anemone. . . . You have to look at the tundra this way, summing up the vast and the intimate."

Writing more than thirty years after Marshall and seeming by his style to be a less effusive, somewhat more urbane personality, Milton nevertheless closely matches the earlier scientist's philosophy and emotions about the arctic wilderness. Milton is well aware of Marshall's dream of securing a wilderness on so vast a scale that people could never fully know it or destroy it. He writes of walking on a high rock ridge:

> *This is wildness on a scale the mountain men once knew in our Far West—a wildness stemming from hundreds of miles of empty land, expanses of unexplored territory, and unnamed mountains, valleys, and rivers. In such terrain, self-reliance is forced upon you by the nature of the land. You adapt to it, not it to you. Man has not yet conquered this country. The wilderness stands on its own, natural and free; it is not propped by "access" roads and rangers, interpretive centers and regulations on use, as in the quasi-wilderness of our national parks. Here there is no prostitution of the freedom so essential to wilderness.*

87

I hope that man continues to have the good sense to allow some of the Earth to go its own way, unmanaged and formally unutilized. In an age when urbanization threatens to engulf most of human life and to absorb man's spirit completely, the wilder parts of the Earth grow ever more important as places where he can relearn what he is and where he came from. Freedom is an empty word, as is solitude, until experienced. Cities, although they offer much else, provide little solitude and freedom for the nourishment of man's soul—at least for my soul.

Like Marshall, Milton touches also upon the theme of humility: "Here, from this little known summit, the world has never seemed so large nor I so inconsequential."

He reiterates, also, Marshall's call for broad preservation:

I hope man has the vision to keep his civilization from at least a few such wildernesses as these—wilderness on the old, vast scale—so that the wolf and caribou may continue to live as they always have; and for their own sake, not ours.

"Recreation," "productivity," "undisturbed gene pool"—all of these concepts should have nothing to do with wilderness such as this. It should be left alone to continue its age-old cycles of life and season. And if this wildness also can be an incidental reservoir for restoring man's spirit, then fine. But that is not the purpose of this place. Its purpose is to be. Man's role should be . . . let it be.

The great difference between Robert Marshall's experiences and John Milton's is that at the time of Milton's trip, men had begun to foul the wilderness. Upon finding the residue of an oil exploration crew, Milton was appalled. He recounts that "the wreckage was littered about with no more thought for those who might follow here than a group of monkeys let loose in a fine French restaurant would feel for the next day's patrons." He concluded:

I don't think wildness precludes man; rather it requires the harmonizing of man with the rest of nature—on nature's terms. . . . In the wilderness, man should be a nomad, an ethical nomad. Why can't man travel through wild country in such a manner that he leaves behind him the least possible traces of his passing? . . . The ethic is simple . . . man is measured by what does not remain.

In wilderness I am free to confront the universe directly, with a minimal veneer of civilization's achievement, and I feel a new perspective, a new proportion. Without it, I am lost. But there is not enough wilderness for everyone and I wonder if we, as a race, aren't lost—lost in a way that, out here, I shall never be lost.

Milton's cry for wilderness by no means rejects civilization. On the contrary, he recommends that counterpoint, the contrast of civilization's cultural refinements with the wilds. He finds exhilaration in going from one extreme to the other instead of compromising, as so many try to do, in suburbia, rural living, or the well-tended landscapes of Europe. "I need both worlds," he owns. "Indeed, the very words 'civilization' and 'wilderness' require each other to have any real meaning." Bob Marshall would have agreed.

With Milton on his arctic walk was Kenneth Brower, who wrote the most monumental book dealing with the Brooks Range. Published in 1971 and entitled *Earth and the Great Weather,* a name drawn from a shaman's song, it is a Friends of the Earth publication, an oversize coffee-table book with high-quality photography. A composite, contrapuntal work, it has twin themes: an account of Brower's walking trip and also a gathering of general information about the Brooks Range. The range's landforms, fauna, people, and exploration are covered, as the book is liberally jewelled with eloquent passages from, among others, Marshall, Crisler, Milton, explorer/ethnologist Knud Rasmussen, writer Farley Mowat, and mountaineer David Roberts, as well as a number of Native expressions. Some excellent photographers got into the range in the 1960s, and illustrations by Wilbur Mills, Bob Waldrop, Gilbert Staender, Pete Martin, Steve Heizer, John Milton, and others provide a first-quality visual interpretation of what the Brooks Range is. This offers a dimension of understanding that had not previously been available in widely published form.

Earth and the Great Weather also contains one of the first explicit published proposals for Brooks Range and Arctic Slope preservation.

Because it offers such a rich and varied literary and visual experience, I feel that the book requires more energy to go through than does straight reading that builds a certain comfortable momentum. One is apt to peruse and pick around in the handsome volume. But it is a great contribution, summed up in Brower's final point:

The Arctic Slope was somewhere before Atlantic Richfield. It was everywhere, the entire world, to the people who called themselves Inuit, the People. They left it unscarred and rich in human associations. We, the Oil People, who are only the latest in a succession of arctic peoples, must somewhere find the grace to leave the Arctic as we found it, adding our own legends and no more, for the next people to pass that way.

More than two decades have passed since *Earth and the Great Weather* appeared. Four new units of the National Park System have been established in the Brooks Range and its environs, and the Arctic National Wildlife Range has been greatly enlarged into an Arctic National Wildlife Refuge, with a complementary Canadian national park adjoining in Yukon Territory. This has been accomplished with a great deal of publicity for the region and the experiences to be had there. Consequently, thousands have walked and floated where only a few had ventured before. Many fine chapters on the Brooks Range are included in books on Alaska and its conservation systems, and journals like John Milton's and Ken Brower's must be many now.

A fine early one of these is "North of Doonerak," by photographer Joseph G. Standart III, who accompanied me on one of my park planning investigations. It was published in a 1977 issue of *Wilderness Camping* magazine. Another, by Barry Lopez, award-winning author of *Arctic Dreams* (1986), appeared in *Outside* magazine in 1981. There, in "In a Country of Light, Among Animals," Lopez explained that, in summer,

> *The light creates, in this winter-hammered landscape, a feeling of compassion, of release from threat, that is almost palpable. Each minute of light is one stolen from a crushing winter. You walk gently, with a sense of how your body breaks the sunshine, are respectful of plants, speak softly. The light is—no other word for it—precious. You are careful near it.*

A slim book published in 1953 contains some of the best-written Alaskan tales I have run across. *Alaskan Tales* is, indeed, its title; its author, Russell Annabel. Chapter Five is the heart-warming story of how a hospitable though starving Nunamiut community and a pilot-hunter helped each other.

A chapter of special beauty forms the final part of Joe McGinniss's *Going to Extremes* (1980). In his superb telling of a journey into an unexplored cranny of the Brooks Range, McGinniss relates with quiet intensity the awe and the rapture to which Marshall alludes. It is of mystical experience that McGinniss writes. I know whereof I speak, as I was with him when, reverently, we entered the cathedral that we found. I remember instinctively doffing my hat.

Another journal, which has become an entire book, examines a solitary traveler's experiences and feelings so minutely that it warrants special note. It is

David J. Cooper's *Brooks Range Passage*, published in 1982, a piece of writing in the wilderness-revering tradition. Dave Cooper, a college student majoring in ecology, walked from Anaktuvuk Pass to the Alatna River, built a raft, and floated down to Allakaket. His diary records his every step, what he saw, felt, feared, loved, contemplated. He is, I believe, the first writer since Cantwell to describe the texture, the tactile qualities of Brooks Range tundra vegetation with such care that even a blind person could see its beauty. Reading his book is a good way to experience the Brooks Range vicariously in all its detail, in a story sensitively and gracefully told.

I am puzzled, however, by Cooper's rationale for how he conducted his journey. Because of his knowledge of wild foods, he planned to live largely off the land, and in some degree did so, but his approach to that was somewhat atavistic and contradictory. He eschewed firearms but took along a bow and arrow; he used only flies for fishing, yet his other gear was modern, though seemingly rather inadequate in view of what is readily available. He was lucky in his weather, for he did not seem prepared for the Brooks Range at its hungry, hypothermal worst. Indeed, he admits that "if this land were to flex its muscles, I would surely be crushed."

It seems unfortunate that Cooper saw fit to write words of encouragement to those who would live off the country, or even supplement their carried food supply to any large extent. Arctic Alaska is a rather bare cupboard; wild foods do not grow just anywhere for an ever-increasing number of visitors to gather. Even the Native people have to know the country intimately to subsist. Cooper hit the blueberry season just right. I have floated the Noatak River when there was scarcely a blueberry left in the country. I was too late. If rain roils the water of a stream, fishing is poor indeed. As for trying to shoot ptarmigan or even parka squirrels, the energy gained might well not equal the energy expended.

To be sure, killing a fat sheep or a caribou could make a huge difference, as it did to Robert Marshall, and even to Kenneth Brower and John Milton, but that is now out of the question. A young man who trapped out of a cabin up the John River one year, living off moose and caribou, told me he could not do it again. The game just wasn't that plentiful anymore. Lois Crisler, writing in the 1950s, rejected the taking of game as a substitute for supplies brought in, even though she half-wished for the fresh meat: "We were here of our own choice, we had come by plane, it was up to us to bring our food. Living off the country in this age is an anachronism, except in real, unavoidable emergency." She was not speaking of the subsistence lifestyle carried on by most Native people and some other bush residents in northern Alaska, of course. That has socioeconomic and cultural roots and ramifications that separate it from the let's-live-off-the-country vacationers or even wilderness researchers.

Brooks Range resources are finite. Willow thickets can be quickly stripped of burnable wood, even if each user is frugal. Recently, I have heard that Noatak trippers, stormbound and backed up at their put-in lake, were severely depleting the fish there, fish that take years to grow in arctic waters. As long as land managers are unable or unwilling to control numbers of people, such resource depletion is disastrously inevitable.

I am sorry, too, that Cooper spoke so lightly about the joys of catch-and-release fishing, alleging it does the fish no harm. Perhaps not. It is an increasingly recommended method of extending the sport, using barbless hooks. I shall leave the question for the fishery biologists to answer, but the grayling is a very delicate fish, and I doubt if its health improves from being caught for fun. I have done it myself, and I worry about it.

The principal contribution of *Brooks Range Passage,* besides sharing David Cooper's inner thoughts, feelings, and experiences, is that it stresses again the need for understanding, to slow down. "Sitting back at the edge of the clearing in the forest, I realize how I appreciate this country the most, and when I derive the maximum amount of understanding from what I see," he writes. "It is when I slow down, when I stop and am with the land."

> *I could fly over the miles or speed through many of them in a motor boat, but that isn't what this country is about. It's one-step-after-another country; it's fully living each and every move between tussocks, planning routes a hundred yards at a time day after day, following streams to their sources, seeing every inch of channels, crossing divides, and following rivers from their trickling origins.... I feel primitive and entirely myself here, living with this land on its own as I make my own way, my own life. The life forms, colors, endless walking in pristine country fill me with incredible satisfaction.*
>
> *What can I give to this country but my understanding of it to other interested people so that they might help it remain wild.*

Two more books have appeared that are based on the experience of living in the wilderness of the Brooks Range. They may be the last, now that much of it is park or refuge, and the solitudes of the north are fading fast. One is *Our Arctic Year* (1984), by Vivian and Gil Staender, he being one of the photographers contributing to *Earth and the Great Weather.* Their story of a year spent in the central Brooks Range, cabin-building and all, is recounted by his wife. The other book, published in 1988, is by Billie Wright's widower, Sam. It is entitled *Koviashuvik,* an Inupiat word meaning "a time and place of joy," and the name of their wilderness home.

The Staenders' book is a brightly written journal, with much dialogue to entertain with the daily events and adventures of wilderness living among pet-named wildlife. The work of philosopher/scientist Wright, written in a striking dancelike, contrapuntal style, also tells of cabin-building and other aspects of wilderness living. But his is a far deeper work of philosophical insight, soul-searching. It invokes the spirit of the Brooks Range, contemplates the wisdom of solitude, probes the very nature of human beings and their carings and questings, their clinging to premises "that had better change or our survival is uncertain." Moving from the mountains to New York, the Southwest, and Great Britain and covering a number of years, Wright the theologian evaluates life and culture from the perspective of the Brooks Range, where "infinity is not a philosophical concept. It is a daily experience."

I was interested to note the contrast between the two authors' treatment of hunting. To Vivian Staender, killing "Mighty Moose" for necessary winter food is a "barbaric" act that reduces her to tears, and she pleads for the life of a "cute," bent-on-destruction bear. To Billie Wright, says Sam, butchering winter's food for the first time was also traumatic for someone whose meat had always come packaged, but "to kill an animal for food is a sacred thing at Koviashuvik. . . . I hunt, kill and butcher our caribou or moose with a quality of excitement and awe because this is the way we lived for millions of years," he explains later.

Physically and psychologically and socially I am a hunter. We are all hunters, even though we have transformed hunting into a sport. Transformed it into games like football, business and war.

At Koviashuvik we have transformed football into wood cutting, and business into food gathering and hunting. We would transform war if we could. Yes we would.

With Robert Marshall, Wright shares the goal of "preservation of these mountains—that there may remain on this continent a wild place where the song of wolves and the migration of caribou may remind us of who we are and from whence we came."

Wright was at Anaktuvuk Pass when the first tractor train came in, bound for the oil developments, and in his book he notes: "All the problems of the modern world came into this small village of inland Eskimos, still dependent on migrating herds of caribou. This was the beginning of the end of a way of life which had sustained the Nunamiut for thousands of years."

Wright spoke out on behalf of "voiceless" wilderness and solitude at the public hearings on the Trans-Alaska Oil Pipeline, and in *Koviashuvik* he reviews his testimony:

> *Who will speak for those of our own species to come, those who will have no place left in the world uncontaminated by their predecessor's self-righteous need to convert everything, including beauty and solitude, into dollars? Who will speak for this last great wilderness to remain wilderness? For if it goes, it will never be returned. I have no choice. I must speak because I am not voiceless, and this is my home. . . .*
>
> *For real progress is to recognize, preserve and wisely use our resources. And our greatest resource in the greatest jeopardy, because it can never be replaced or recreated, is wilderness. . . . Our common responsibility, in the light of overwhelming scientific and technical evidence . . . is to save the wilderness. . . . When it goes, there is no other.*

Wright's testimony heralded the first of two important books telling the story of the Arctic National Wildlife Refuge (ANWR) and the struggle to keep it oil-free. *Vanishing Arctic*, which came out in 1988, is a handsome picture book illustrated by two distinguished Alaska photographers, Wilbur Mills and Art Wolfe.

The text, by T. H. Watkins, is a marriage of sensitive and eloquent description and an impressive marshalling of facts about "a land of enormous geometry etched by the cutting edge of light. Implacable, raw, elemental, beautiful. And threatened."

"Oil *versus* wilderness. It is an old story by now, one whose narrative has filled a million pages," writes historian Watkins. "But rarely have the lines of discord been drawn with greater exactitude, rarely if ever have the stakes been so high, and never has conflict erupted in a landscape more powerful than the fragile magnificence that lies at the top of the world."

Watkins, who is editor of The Wilderness Society's *Wilderness* magazine, interweaves the story of the refuge with interludes of a journey through it. Then he tackles "The Problem"—the grisly fate of a life-sustaining land with oil addiction hanging over it—and an Inupiat asks him, "When the oil is gone, what you gonna do?"

The following year Wolfe teamed up with the Alaskan author/planner Art Davidson to bring out another, bigger picture book, *Alakshak, the Great Country*, with a good story of an ANWR journey.

Yet another one is in Larry Rice's book of Alaska wilderness journeys, *Gathering Paradise* (1990). That story, however, not only touches on the oil development debate but also gives a sobering account of what it is like to travel the

Arctic in bone-chilling fog and sleet, to have feet suffering from constant wetness and cold, again and again to encounter bears, and to have a food and fuel cache rifled, not by animals but by recently arrived humans—a mortal crime akin to horse thievery in the Old West! In a tandem account of plunging down the rapid Killik River through "great footloose country," Rice contraposes the hum of distant oil rigs "in an environmentally up-for-grabs world" with entering silence "a million years thick."

The second work devoted entirely to the oil-threatened refuge is Debbie S. Miller's *Midnight Wilderness,* also published in 1990. Miller is an Alaskan with thirteen years' experience of hiking, climbing, and kayaking in what she terms "the essence of America's wilderness heritage." Writing straightforwardly, but also sensitively, she not only recites the story of ANWR well but also shares the rewards of the wilderness hiker: "the gifts of nature and a greater appreciation of life."

Miller is a teacher as well as a seasoned writer, and her book is a teacherly one, deftly explaining the whys of the forces that have made and affect a country as yet neither "manipulated, conquered or consumed," and where animals outnumber man. After reading *Midnight Wilderness,* one is not only entertained but also extremely well informed about this ecosystem on which millions of lives depend, including thousands of human lives. Her work is reminiscent of the nature writing of U.S. Supreme Court Justice William O. Douglas in noting all the interesting floral and wildlife events along a day's march.

Never self-consciously instructive or condescending but always enlightening and appreciative, Miller knows "the spirit of pure wildness, in such an awesome land, that lingers on in our hearts and minds." She recounts a walk with her husband Dennis on which "there were no footprints, no signs of old campsites, no candy bar wrappers, no plastic. Even if others had walked our exact route, there was still that exhilarating sensation that we may have walked in places where perhaps no human had ever set foot."

But her book has a more somber mission; it tells a tale of menacing likelihood: the old, old story of birthright and pottage, as the life center of this world-class refuge lies bound on the altar of oil. Miller unsheets the corpse of landscape she charges arctic oil development with having ravaged just west of the refuge. She reminds the world of the "sacred quality about this ground . . . America's greatest wildlife mecca"—not only calving place of the emblematic caribou but also a destination to which hundreds of other species travel thousands of miles to breed.

Midnight Wilderness encourages reflection on the meaning of Earth itself, and, in a lovely preface, Margaret Murie joins Miller in calling for the courage to protect the region, not only for future humanity but also "for the sake of *the land itself* . . . empty of technology and full of life."

ARCTIC REFUGE, YUKON PARK

That is the finest place of its kind I have ever seen. It is a complete eco-system, needs nothing man can take to it except complete protection from his own transgression.

—George L. Collins

Except for official reports and stories of hunting and other forms of physical adventure, most Brooks Range literature—at least until recently—has dwelt on the theme of wilderness appreciation. And it has paralleled and supported a growing concern for conservation in the Alaskan north.

It was Bob Marshall, of course, who first trumpeted the call for Brooks Range protection, but the first successful effort to that end was not made in the country that he had explored and extolled. Rather, it focused on an area farther east, where the mountains reach their apogee close to the arctic seacoast, and where the wildlife is most evident.

Since the 1920s, wildlife biologist Olaus Murie had been urging patient understanding of that country. He and his brother Adolph had mushed in the Brooks Range and had spread word of its biotic and geographic glories. As he was later to write of its conservation, "The idea, not yet understood by all, was to protect permanently another portion of our planet for sensitive people to go and get acquainted with themselves, to enjoy untouched nature, and to leave the lovely, unmarked country as they find it."

The story of the Arctic National Wildlife Refuge, originally called the Arctic National Wildlife Range, is well told by one at the root of it all, George L. Collins, then a senior planner for the National Park Service. He was, in the early 1950s, the service's representative on the Federal Field Committee for Development Planning

Caribou in Atigun Gorge, Arctic National Wildlife Refuge. (Photograph by Gil Mull)

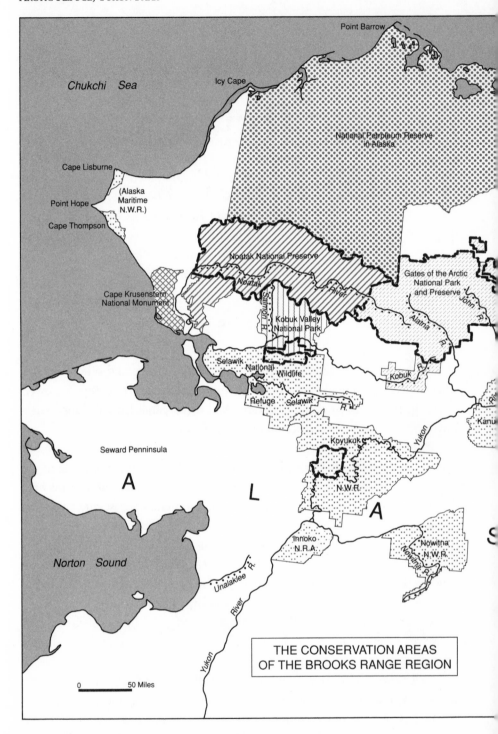

Point Barrow

Chukchi Sea

Icy Cape

National Petroleum Reserve in Alaska

Cape Lisburne

(Alaska Maritime N.W.R.)

Point Hope

Cape Thompson

Noatak National Preserve

Gates of the Arctic National Park and Preserve

Noatak

Salmon R.

River

John R.

Alatna R.

Cape Krusenstern National Monument

Kobuk Valley National Park

Kobuk R.

Selawik National

Wildlife

Refuge

Selawik

Selawik R.

Kanu

Koyukuk

Yukon

Seward Penninsula

N.W.R.

A

L

A

S

Innoko N.R.A.

Nowitna N.W.R.

Nowitna

Norton Sound

Unalakleet R.

River

Yukon

0   50 Miles

THE CONSERVATION AREAS
OF THE BROOKS RANGE REGION

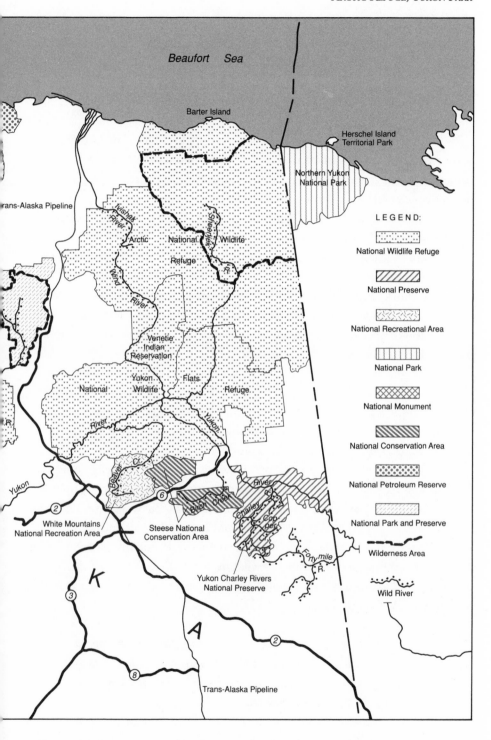

Beaufort Sea

Barter Island

Herschel Island
Territorial Park

Northern Yukon
National Park

Trans-Alaska Pipeline

Kishak River

Arctic National Wildlife

Sheenjek R.

Refuge

Wind River

Venetie
Indian
Reservation

Yukon Wildlife   Flats

National   Refuge.

River

Yukon

LEGEND:

National Wildlife Refuge

National Preserve

National Recreational Area

National Park

National Monument

National Conservation Area

National Petroleum Reserve

National Park and Preserve

Wilderness Area

Wild River

Beaver Cr.

(2)

(6)

Birch Creek

River

Charley

Copper Cr.

Fortymile R.

White Mountains
National Recreation Area

Steese National
Conservation Area

Yukon Charley Rivers
National Preserve

K

(3)

A

(2)

(8)

Trans-Alaska Pipeline

99

in Alaska, and he had been heading an Alaskan Recreation Survey, an outgrowth of a 1949 Alaska Science Conference and a project encouraged by the service's director, Conrad L. Wirth. "Go to Alaska and see that great piece of the world," Wirth had told Collins. The planner thought of the National Park System in terms of an organized, thematic approach to preserving and interpreting America's great natural and historical heritage.

The Arctic essentially was awesome and impenetrable, from the standpoint of the recreation survey, Collins later recalled. As he pondered his approach to arctic conservation, the secretary of the Arctic Institute of North America, Joseph Flakne, became concerned lest wilderness values be forgotten amid a burgeoning interest in oil exploration in arctic Alaska. He enlisted the aid of Olaus Murie, who had become director of The Wilderness Society, and began corresponding with Starker Leopold, chairman of the Sierra Club's Natural Sciences Committee, as well as with Collins and his biologist colleague, Lowell Sumner.

Collins talked with two senior officials of the Geological Survey: Alaska Branch Chief George Gates and John C. Reed, another Alaska expert in Washington, D.C. "I want to get into the Arctic," Collins said to Reed. "There's no great national park in the Arctic anywhere that I know of."

"If you stay east of Pet 4 [then the Naval Petroleum Reserve Number 4 on the Arctic Slope, now the National Petroleum Reserve in Alaska], there's nothing over there until you get to the Mackenzie Delta in the Yukon. . . . You'll be out of our hair, and that's where the finest relief, the highest mountains in the Alaskan arctic, and the greatest landscapes are," Reed replied.

"He opened my eyes to a vision that was way beyond anything I'd had before," Collins recalled. "He assumed I was after a national park somewhere up there. I wasn't necessarily. I just wanted to see what the score was. But when John Reed told me that, then I reported to George Gates. He said 'Sure. Why not?' He was all for it."

But Collins soon did begin to think about a park, not only a national park but a great international one, for to wildlife, the U.S.–Canada boundary was meaningless. "No one had ever thought about any gigantic things going across into both countries," Collins noted.

> We saw the fallacy of having a park, or whatever you want to call the area, divided by an international boundary when you had so many migratory species, both marine and terrestrial, that used both sides of the line. It was one habitat.
>
> We didn't know what to call it. We used such terms as "conservation reserve," or "preserve," or "conservation area." Generi-

*cally, it was a park to us, always, and still is. . . . The scenery was
enthralling. It was simply stupendous, beyond description, absolutely
magnificent. And we wanted to go out to sea, taking in the habitat of
the beluga whales and the migratory creatures that live by land and sea
both. . . . We didn't take in any of it [the coastal waters] because we
didn't know how to do it. We didn't know enough about it. I wish now
that we had just arbitrarily taken in a chunk.*

Anxious to keep away from the geologists' turf, Collins and his NPS partner Lowell Sumner stayed east of the Canning River in their field investigations, and they had good support from the scientists at the navy's Arctic Research Laboratory and among their Geological Survey friends. "There was never any question as to whether what Doc Sumner and I were undertaking to do in exploring out there at the east end of the Brooks Range was worth doing," said Collins. "Rather, the question was, 'Where have you been all these years? Why haven't you been in here a long time ago?' They were delighted."

In 1952, he and Sumner camped at Lake Schrader with a Geological Survey party, checked out the Sheenjek River country on the south side of the range, and visited the commissioner of Yukon Territory. For a time, they had the aid of Leopold and the eminent Scottish ecologist Sir F. Fraser Darling. These two were quick to urge wilderness protection in Alaska's far north. Their book, *Wildlife in Alaska,* sponsored by the New York Zoological Society and the Conservation Foundation, came out the following year. Their sponsors endorsed the scientists' finding that the eastern end of the Brooks Range, which descends to the coastal plain on the north and the Yukon Valley on the south, would be an extremely important wilderness area. "Not only would such a reservation serve to maintain a sample of the primitive northland for posterity," Leopold and Darling pointed out, "but it could be a base for long-term ecological studies of the Arctic flora and fauna. The scientific importance of reserving such study areas cannot be overemphasized."

Collins and Sumner returned to the Brooks Range in 1953 with landscape architect William Carnes of the NPS and archaeologist Alex Richardelli, a graduate student at Columbia University. They flew the territory at low level, checking on the Porcupine caribou herd, and investigated the Firth River–Joe Creek region in the Alaska–Yukon border country. Then, with Marvin Mangus of the USGS to help them, Sumner, Carnes, and Richardelli floated the tumultuous Kongakut River.

Mangus, a veteran arctic ridge-runner who later was to help bring in the first Prudhoe Bay oil well, remembers with amusement that the two park men seemed to him like Boy Scouts on an outing. So excited were they in their adventures that

Carnes inadvertently had had the wrong supply barrels flown in to the Kongakut. As a result, said Mangus, they had a huge supply of toilet paper but no oars for the foldboats. They lined and floated the river a few hundred yards at a time. Out of food and weathered in at their aircraft pickup site, they walked by compass to the coast.

Director Murie of The Wilderness Society published an article on Collins's and Sumner's investigations in the winter 1953–1954 issue of *The Living Wilderness*, as did the Sierra Club in its *Bulletin*. "The northeast Arctic wilderness offers an ideal chance to preserve an undisturbed natural area large enough to be biologically self-sufficient," wrote Sumner and Collins, adding prophetically that "the Arctic wilderness is easier to reach today than was the Yellowstone forty or more years ago. . . . There is still time to preserve it for scientific study and public enjoyment." But the word was already out around the conservation circuit. At its 1953 annual meeting, the Federation of Western Outdoor Clubs resolved to support an effort to create an arctic wilderness preserve.

In 1956, the New York Zoological Society, The Conservation Foundation, The Wilderness Society, and the University of Alaska teamed up to send Olaus and Margaret Murie back to the northland they knew and loved for a summer of further research. This time the Muries had the company and assistance of graduate students Bob Krear and George Schaller and of Brina Kessel, a professor of zoology at the University of Alaska.

During their stay in the Sheenjek Valley, the group entertained another prominent conservation leader, Justice Douglas, for whom, briefly, the reserve that was now being proposed was to be named. His experiences there became the opening chapter in his book *My Wilderness—the Pacific West*, published in 1960. "This is a loneliness that is joyous and exhilarating," he wrote. "Not a place to possess . . . it is one to behold with wonderment. . . . This last American living wilderness must remain sacrosanct . . . the place for man turned scientist and explorer, poet and artist. Here he can experience a new reverence for life that is outside his own and yet a vital and joyous part of it."

George Collins praised the work of the Muries in furthering the idea of a protected arctic wilderness. Richard Watt declared in a thesis on its recreational potential that probably no one had worked harder to support the establishment of the Arctic National Wildlife Range than Olaus Murie. The wide respect he had earned and his ability to communicate with "both the common man and the accomplished politician" were, said Watt, largely responsible for Murie's success, and "certainly much credit for the [acceptance of a proposed] Arctic Wildlife Range rightly belongs to Dr. Murie." Alaskans seemed to be responsive to Murie's call—the Alaska Federation of Women's Clubs, the Fairbanks Garden Club, and the Fairbanks

Chamber of Commerce as well. The Tanana Valley Sportsmen's Association swung from opposition to support, and the Fairbanks *News-Miner* gave its editorial blessing. The territorial governor welcomed the possibility. Nationally, the National Wildlife Federation and the Izaak Walton League added their applause to Secretary of the Interior Fred A. Seaton's stated intention of doing something to protect the area.

But what kind of a reserve should there be, and who should administer it? The National Park Service was too preoccupied with other interests and concerns to seize upon the idea of a remote arctic park, even though the director was sympathetic to the concept. More important, the realization grew upon proponents of arctic conservation that something other than classic national park status was needed. Murie worried about the possibility of overdevelopment for recreation if national park designation came about. George Collins himself, having realized that protection which ruled out traditional prospecting and hunting might be difficult, became part of a consensus that strict park status was not a wise goal to pursue. "We had indigenous people in the area," he explained. "We had a tradition of hunting and prospecting. We had international interests to consider. . . . It was felt in the service and in the department, I think, that national park status wasn't quite the thing for this one."

At a Wilderness Conference in San Francisco in 1957, which Collins chaired, he met with Edward Woozley, director of the Bureau of Land Management, administrator of the area that included the Brooks Range; with the regional director of the Fish and Wildlife Service, Clarence Rhode; and with such leading conservationists as the Muries and Richard and Doris Leonard of the Sierra Club. They all decided that wildlife range status would be the best, the simplest, the least controversial, the most fitting for the area. They probably also realized that it was the most likely way to protect the area, considering the legislative requirements for authorizing a national park.

Preparatory to a public land order establishing an Arctic National Wildlife Range, legislation was introduced in Congress to limit mining to subsurface rights only, and thus protect wildlife habitats. However, in 1959, Alaska was awarded statehood and blocked the measure. It wanted nothing to impede mining interests, nor was the chauvinistic new state desirous of having a specialized federal fief in the north. But Secretary of the Interior Seaton had strong public support for a range, and he had Clarence Rhode, an Alaskan of great charm and devotion to the resources, at his side. Rhode had given the secretary a personal tour, and Seaton became sold on the range idea.

103

On December 6, 1960, after seeing the congressional bills die, and not long before he left office, Seaton signed Public Land Order 2214, creating the range and closing it to mining activities. (It would remain open to oil and gas exploration and development but under stipulations and controls.) The state of Alaska tried to get Seaton's successor, Stewart L. Udall, to rescind the order, but after careful review, Secretary Udall upheld it. Alaska took revenge by holding up appropriations for the range for almost nine years. Eventually, however, Congress began supplying money for it, thus giving the executive action a legislative blessing.

The Arctic National Wildlife Range, bigger than Connecticut and Massachusetts combined, became, in a way, a magnificent memorial to two of the men who had done much to bring it about. It had received the life of Clarence Rhode, whose airplane crashed among its mountains in 1958. Olaus Murie, who had studied and promulgated it so lovingly, died in 1963.

The Arctic National Wildlife Range in Alaska was accomplished, but the international reserve was not. That effort went on. Collins retired from the National Park Service in 1960 and joined with his friends Doris and Richard Leonard and Dorothy Varian in founding Conservation Associates. As consultants, they were adept at getting along with industry and making it accept with good grace some of its environmental follies. At first, their efforts were bent toward fending off gas pipelines aimed across the Arctic Slope or through the valleys of the Arctic National Wildlife Range itself. They had not forgotten the dream of international protection for the caribou herd and other wildlife, however.

In 1968, the first discovery oil well at Prudhoe Bay came in, and change exploded across western arctic America. "The Arctic was no longer a mysterious romantic neverland, unknown and feared," mused Collins. "It became the hard-bitten scene of economic controversy, of lost hopes and new dreams. And there we were in the middle of it all between Alaska and Canada, with a voice bleating about saving wilderness."

Land claims of the Alaskan Native people stood in the way of oil and gas development. The United States government had never made a settlement with them. Secretary of the Interior Udall, sympathetic to Native concerns and diligent in his responsibilities as principal federal land steward, had, in 1966, closed off the selection of all Alaskan federal land for state and private ownership until Native claims could be settled. Congress addressed this with the Alaska Native Claims Settlement Act of 1971, a blueprint for dividing the huge federally owned Alaska pie among Native, state, and federal interests so that such matters as the Trans-Alaska Oil Pipeline could proceed without embroilment in land claims.

As the Native claims legislation first began to take form, in 1969, Robert Weeden, president of the Alaska Conservation Society, summoned representatives of some seventy Alaska conservation groups and government agencies to a landmark conference in Juneau for a "wilderness workshop" that resulted in formation of the Alaska Wilderness Council to push for the setting aside of more wilderness preserves in the national forests and other Alaskan areas. Joseph Fitzgerald, chairman of the Federal Field Committee for Development Planning in Alaska, asked the council to document what Alaskan lands should become new national parks and wildlife refuges. And on a Washington, D.C., visit the next year, David Hickok, a resource specialist with the field committee, suggested to Senate Interior Committee staff counsel William Van Ness that a provision be put in the Native claims legislation directing the secretary of the interior to make park and refuge recommendations.

That provision eventually became Section 17 (d) (2) of the Native Claims Settlement Act, specifying that eighty million acres be looked at, with recommendations due in two years. Conservationists, led by Edgar Wayburn, president of the Sierra Club, had urged twice that acreage. Despite all the efforts of conservation lobbyists and the mighty bipartisan help of Congressmen Morris K. Udall of Arizona and John P. Saylor of Pennsylvania, the provision was at first knocked out in the House of Representatives by opponents charging "lock-up." It passed in the Senate, however, with the powerful backing of Senators Henry Jackson of Washington, Gaylord Nelson of Wisconsin, and Alan Bible of Nevada. Bible, who chaired the Senate Subcommittee on National Parks and Recreation, had a firsthand understanding of the conservation opportunities, thanks to an Alaskan tour given him by National Park Service Director George B. Hartzog, Jr., accompanied by Dr. and Mrs. Wayburn.

The Senate provision added authority to recommend additions to the National Wild and Scenic Rivers System, a suggestion made by the Sierra Club's Alaskan representative, Jack Hession. New national forest areas were provided for in the Senate–House conference ironing out the differences in the respective bills. Therefore, Section 17 (d) (2) of the act reserved what came to be termed d-2 lands, to be studied for possible inclusion in four federal land management systems, usually referred to henceforth as the Four Systems.

There was also another section, 17 (d)(1), calling for the identification of other lands to be retained in federal ownership for public purposes. Some of these d-1 lands, totaling forty-five million acres, were to end up helping to round out the protection of the ecosystems encompassed in the proposed new or enlarged parks and wildlife refuges.

The federal land management agencies and the conservationists had been very busy identifying what lands should be reserved for parks and refuges. The wildlife biologists knew that the existing Arctic National Wildlife Range, big as it was, did not adequately cover (and still does not) the full range of the Porcupine caribou herd and other wildlife.

Proposals for a much-enlarged range would extend it westward across the Marsh Fork of the Canning River and the upper Ivishak almost to Atigun Pass and the Trans-Alaska Oil Pipeline corridor, taking in much of the Philip Smith Mountain

Mount Chamberlin dominates the Franklin Mountains in the Arctic National Wildlife Refuge. Recent map revisions indicate it to be the highest peak in the Brooks Range—9,020 feet above sea level. (Photograph by Wilbur Mills)

Range. This was north of the Arctic (and Continental) Divide. South of that, a huge territory was additionally proposed, including the watersheds of the Wind, Junjik, Koness, Sheenjek, and Coleen rivers, and part of the Porcupine. Much of this was proposed to be designated as Wilderness, as was all of the old range.

Only the old range, minus much of its coastal plain, actually received official Wilderness status, the other proposals being beaten down politically both before and after the Alaska National Interest Lands Conservation Act of 1980 that finally authorized, by legislation, the huge systems of protected resources in the Great Land.

The upper Ivishak, upper Sheenjek, and Wind rivers were accorded National Wild River status, but the Porcupine, also proposed, was relegated to a list for further study. As finally established, the renamed Arctic National Wildlife Refuge was somewhat pared down in the western Philip Smith Mountains, and was deeply indented by the Venetie Indian Reservation as well as by a long block of state-selected land thrusting in from the Canadian border. This was finally relinquished to the refuge. The refuge was never permitted to include Chandalar and Big lakes, keys to the Philip Smith Mountains, because of mining claims and other state interests.

Nevertheless, the refuge now is more than double the size of the old range. Moreover, it was made to adjoin the concurrently established Yukon Flats National Wildlife Refuge, not only including part of the Yukon River itself but also the lower Sheenjek and Porcupine. Reservation of a utility corridor across the Arctic Refuge for a possible gas pipeline was dropped by agreement between President Jimmy Carter and Prime Minister Pierre Trudeau in favor of a route following either the oil pipeline or the Alaska Highway.

Great as was the accomplishment in Alaska, the dream of an international refuge was yet unrealized. In 1969, George Collins had met Dr. Andrew R. Thompson of the University of British Columbia Faculty of Law. They were attending a conference in Edmonton, Alberta, titled "Productivity and Conservation in Northern Circumpolar Lands," an excellent occasion for promulgating international wildlife protection. Thompson and Collins decided to sponsor an Arctic International Wildlife Range Conference, which was held in Whitehorse, in Yukon Territory, the next year, and, following a suggestion from Canada's Minister of Indian Affairs and Northern Development, Jean Cretien, established the Arctic International Wildlife Range Society. This became loosely affiliated with the Canadian Wildlife Federation and enjoyed much goodwill and support both in Canada and the United States. The federation called in much of this support in 1974 for a meeting in Ottawa with senior Canadian bureaucrats. Collins later recalled that the Canadians were courteous but not enthusiastic, perhaps a little embarrassed by the occasion. Apparently, Canada was not yet ready to let wildlife interests interfere with potential oil and gas development. Cretien's promise at the 1970 conference, "I will do everything possible to establish the range," was being tempered.

The suggestion that the northern part of the Yukon Territory be set aside as a wildlife range had the support of the Native people there, however. A special commission, the Mackenzie Valley Pipeline Inquiry, headed by British Columbia Supreme Court Justice Thomas R. Berger, had listened to the Natives' concerns over gas and oil development with care and solicitude. Accordingly, the Indians of Old Crow asked that a wildlife range protect their hunting grounds. Such a range—the size proposed at the 1970 Whitehorse conference—would embrace all lands in Yukon Territory north of the Porcupine, Bell, and Little Bell rivers, matching in size the Alaskan range, and large enough to encompass most of Canada's portion of the winter and summer range of the great Porcupine caribou herd.

In his bold, comprehensive report, the first part of which came out late in 1976, Justice Berger showed that he saw, understood, and respected the Native viewpoint. He adopted and advanced the wildlife range idea so magnificently, that, to quote Collins, "it electrified the whole country up there. . . . At that level of thought and action . . . people looked and listened. That commission very quickly developed within itself, in its own right, a conservation outlook, perspective, and determination never before witnessed in northwest Canada." It reinforced three important points made at the 1970 conference by economist Peter H. Pearse of the University of British Columbia:

> *The advocates of change and the native people themselves must recognize that the traditional way of life, once destroyed, can never be reconstructed. Any proposal for development in the Arctic is unlikely to be successful unless it can be shown to benefit not only the nation as a whole but also the specific communities most directly affected. A wild species cannot be protected by preservation of only part of its required range or habitat. Wilderness preserved in very small units is meaningless.*

Despite the emphasis on wilderness, the international range advocates hoped to work cooperatively with industry to protect the Arctic, not to defy the oil and gas interests. Much like the approach to establishing the range in Alaska, the strict wilderness park idea was modified in favor of management more akin to multiple use. Because wildlife habitat preservation meant maintaining general wilderness conditions, proponents seemed to feel that if industry could be enlightened, it would somehow temper its activities to fit gently into an otherwise undisturbed environment. Arthur M. Pearson of the Canadian Wildlife Service, speaking at the Whitehorse conference, reminded his listeners that "the wildlife in northern Yukon is in delicate balance with its environment, and activity by man that does not recognize that fact and adjust accordingly, will produce disastrous results."

Noting that serious ecological damage in the Arctic could be irreversible, Peter Pearse complained that large outlays for geological and engineering studies had not been matched by money for studies of the biological resources. "Experience suggests that apparently innocuous actions often have profound and lasting effects on ecological conditions," said Pearse, who later became commissioner of Yukon Territory. The economist held that past ecological damage had often been unnecessary, the result of ignorance, and that with clear standards and incentives to do better, industry would comply, even at higher cost, to avoid criticism. "By providing legal status for the area which ensures recognition of non-industrial values, attention will be focused on the need to protect these other values," he said. "Explicit standards of development will then become essential, and within these rules industry can proceed with certainty." He warned that "multiple use is not a panacea for resource development problems."

That did not prevent another conference speaker, Edward L. Patton, president of the Alyeska Pipeline Service Company, from favoring a multiple-use approach to arctic development and conservation; he said that the oil industry was willing to meet the test of safeguarding natural values.

George Collins was disturbed by the ogreish requirements of the oil industry, however. He emphasized that "the range is needed because there is no other region of the North American Arctic that still exhibits, comparatively unchanged, so wide a range of land forms and native life." But he added:

> *The point is to get industry to acknowledge realistically the intrinsic value of the scenery, wildlife, water, air, and man in the proposed wildlife range as well as it already has [recognized] the earth-resources industry claims elsewhere in the Arctic. It is hoped that industry can help in protecting those cultural resources, their natural processes of evolution, even at some lessening here and there of profits, as a major part of industry's own responsibility, aided by all the rest of us in science, government, and other walks of life. Through such a cooperative course, but in no other way, can future conservation in the Arctic be realized now that exploitative industry is there in force.*

Collins and Conservation Associates prided themselves on getting along with industry, talking things out frankly, for they found a number of top industrialists sympathetic to conservation goals. "We like them. We can deal with them," Collins remarked. "We always let them know, found some way to let them know of our disapproval, and still were able to keep on good terms and talk it out." Industry did begin to hear and heed environmentalist outcries and consequent government monitoring. It had backed down on an arctic coastal pipeline route as productivity in the Mackenzie Delta region became questionable, and as great opposition toward industry from conservation groups became apparent.

In some cases, however, industry remained arrogantly scornful and hostile to protests in the name of ecology. And perhaps some on the side of wilderness and wildlife were naive—Little Red Ridinghoods identifying the oil industry with Grandma. This seems evident in a current knock-down-drag-out fight over whether or not industry, albeit on promises of tiptoeing, should enter the coastal plain calving grounds of the great Porcupine caribou herd in the Arctic National Wildlife Refuge. Huge oil reserves are said to be there—enough to last the United States for at least 180 days. At risk, it is also said, is a wondrous wildlife continuum thousands of years old on which thousands of people yet depend, a resource that, if destroyed or even seriously impaired, can never be restored. Mardy Murie has called it "the most precious piece of our country."

In Canada, however, hopes for oil and gas in the arctic Yukon were fading. The Dempster Highway, punched up to the Mackenzie Delta in anticipation of industrial needs that were not to materialize, was seen to have been a folly. The Berger Report had illuminated the significance of an international wildlife range, and a new minister of Indian and northern affairs, the Canadian equivalent of the U.S. secretary of the interior, had taken office. He was Hugh Faulkner, sympathetic to wildlife and wilderness preservation in the Arctic on an international treaty basis. He was also much interested in the U.S. concept of wild rivers, and convened a special conference in Jasper National Park to discuss such a program for Canada.

Having the same general powers of land reservation as has the secretary of the interior, and with the approval of the prime minister, Faulkner, in 1978, withdrew the entire northern Yukon from development pending wilderness park studies and settlement of Native land claims.

George Collins exulted that when conservation action did come to the Yukon at last, it came with a bang. Well, almost. The Northern Yukon National Park was established by the Canadian Parliament as part of a 1984 Final Agreement with the Inuvialuit (the Inuit people of the region), and the wilderness park idea was adopted. "The planning for the National Park and the management thereof shall have as their objects to protect the wilderness characteristics of the area, maintaining its present undeveloped state to the greatest extent possible, and to protect and manage the wildlife population and the wildlife habitat within the area," the agreement stated. It also established the Herschel Island Territorial Park, to be managed no less stringently than the federal area, and a Wildlife Management Advisory Council was set up as well.

The new national park, however, comprises only the northwest quadrant of the huge territory that was withdrawn by Faulkner and is still withdrawn. The park, adjoining Alaska, lies wholly north of the Arctic Divide and west of the Babbage River. Nevertheless, the rest of Yukon Territory's north slope—east of the Babbage—was demarked in the agreement as a special management area wherein development would be strictly controlled.

Directly south of the park, across the Arctic Divide west of Black Fox Creek and down as far as the Old Crow River, a proposed southern component of the Northern Yukon National Park is proposed. In its turn, it must await a final land agreement between Canada and the Council for Yukon Indians, with the territorial government also involved. The matter is progressing slowly, but if Gwich'in sentiments of recent years hold true, wildlife and habitat protection should receive strong support.

Farther east in the rest of the area under withdrawal—south of the Arctic Divide and extending to the border of Northwest Territories, the Canadian Wildlife Service is studying the possibility of a Canadian Wildlife Area under Native–federal–territorial administration.

Meanwhile, as that idea comes under discussion, the International Porcupine Caribou Board has been established to counsel the United States and Canada on the conservation, management, and research involving the great international Porcupine caribou herd. Founded in 1987 through an executive agreement between the two nations (not by a treaty as had long been hoped), the eight-member board represents local, state/territorial, and national interests in its membership. Though without decision-making powers, the advisory group's influence may well control the destiny of one of the world's greatest wildlife resources.

Frigid Crags, at the North Fork of the Koyukuk River, form one of the Gates of the Arctic.
(National Park Service photograph by the author)

KNOCKING AT THE GATES

Here is a GREAT LAND! A raw, untamed, endless expanse, where beyond the comforts and protections of the cities and roadways only the self-reliant are found, facing nature on her own terms. Here is a place where man is judged by what he is, not by what he has. Here is America's last frontier, and the only truly expansive wilderness remaining under the U.S. flag.

—Roger Allin

Protective interest in arctic Alaska first focused on the eastern Brooks Range, which was, after all, the highest part and closest to the coast, and involved international conservation opportunities as well. Bob Marshall's central Brooks Range was not forgotten, however.

One man in particular remembered. He was Roger Allin of the U.S. Fish and Wildlife Service, who arrived in Alaska late in 1950. Although his specialty was freshwater fisheries biology (he was the first such scientist to be sent to Alaska), he soon was pitching in to help colleagues in all manner of duties that fell to his understaffed agency in the north. "I learned the Brooks Range intimately on both sides by doing game counts with wildlife biologists and wolf hunts with predator control people," Allin has recalled.

Exploring whenever he could, until he had flown over almost every part of Alaska, Allin developed as top priorities three areas that "just had to be saved for

113

posterity." One was the Wood River–Tikchik Lakes region, now one of the world's greatest state parks. A second was what has become Lake Clark National Park and Preserve. The third was the Arrigetch Peaks–John River region of the central Brooks Range. In all, Allin analyzed some twenty outstanding Alaskan areas and thus attracted the attention of George Collins, who borrowed Allin for reconnaissance work. Collins invited Allin to go to work for him, and so began a distinguished National Park Service career. Roger Allin was the catalyst who brought about the deep Alaskan commitment of Theodor R. Swem, who first visited the Great Land with him in 1962. A decade later, Assistant Director Ted Swem was to lead the service's Alaska study efforts that would double the size of the National Park System. He also was to head the Alaska Planning Group, which was made up of the federal agencies involved in overall Alaskan conservation allocations.

In 1966, Allin prepared an in-house report on his recommendations for the Park Service, urging more NPS presence in the Forty-Ninth State. Entitled "Alaska: A Plan for Action," the report was couched in stirring terms. "Alaska is of such unique and outstanding character as to qualify in its entirety as a National Park," Allin wrote.

> *Its spectacular land forms, its majestic mountains, the vast expanses of tundra and forests, the innumerable fresh water sparkling lakes and streams, its abundance of game and fish, and the uniqueness of the additional personal freedoms found on this fringe of civilization, provide experiences, while commonplace in Alaska, not duplicated anywhere else in the United States or perhaps the world.*

Then he focused on the Brooks Range:

> *This is raw, uninhabited, undeveloped nature at its best. Here is a place to prove one's worth. With the exception of a cabin or two it is a true wilderness, used only by sportsmen or wilderness seekers. While in this part of Alaska nature is a tough and unforgiving adversary, here also she is beautiful beyond all description—remote, pristine, undiscovered and unspoiled.*

By the time Allin's report was submitted, other voices in and out of government had been raised to urge Alaskan conservation in general and further Brooks Range protection in particular. The republication of Bob Marshall's Brooks Range adventures had been timely.

In 1961, Robert Weeden, president of the Alaska Conservation Society, had called for a new Alaskan policy stating that nothing should allow the wilderness to deteriorate. Writing in *Alaska Sportsman,* he concluded,

> *All who love Alaska have one basic conviction in common. They like Alaska because it is tremendously big and beautiful, our last real wilderness frontier. We must accept the fact that the great Alaskan wilderness itself is our dominant resource. . . . Let us think what such a policy could mean to Alaska, the nation, and to the world.*

In 1963, the governing council of The Wilderness Society that Marshall had helped to found met in Alaska and agreed to explore informally with Secretary of the Interior Udall the classification of a suitable part of the central Brooks Range as Wilderness. Udall strongly believed in parks. Being particularly sanguine about Alaska, he engaged Norman G. Dyhrenfurth, leader of the American Mount Everest Expedition 1963 and a professional cinematographer, to make a documentary film on Alaska's parklands. At first he thought in terms of total coverage of the state to show the American people the glories of what they really had in Alaska. He concluded, however, that such might amount to lobbying Congress and could well offend the chauvinistic state, so he restricted the film to existing National Park System units there. Even so, the award-winning film "Magnificence in Trust" helped focus attention on Alaska's glories. I have always been thankful that his decision, that summer of 1964, was somewhat delayed in reaching the group that was engaged in the film-making and was already on a statewide reconnaissance trip. I was part of that group, being a special assistant to the director of the National Park Service and assigned to be scriptwriter and liaison with NPS and the Interior Department people in Alaska. Thanks to the delay, I saw the Brooks Range for the first time, flying around Mount Igikpak and the Arrigetch Peaks in one mind-blowing day.

Back in Washington, D.C., after that memorable Alaska experience, I was soon helping to edit "Operation Great Land," the report of a distinguished task force on Alaska chaired by George Collins and including consultants Doris Leonard and Sigurd Olson, as well as Robert Luntey, an old NPS Alaska hand.

The Park Service's new director, George Hartzog, had Udall's blessing to be aggressive in seeking to preserve while opportunities existed. Alaska's scenery had been, of course, extolled since early in the century. George Collins' Alaska Recreation Survey of 1955 had been introduced by Alaska's territorial governor, who urged that the territory's recreational heritage be preserved. The Outdoor Recreation Resources

Review Commission had published a special Alaskan report in 1962. Now, three years later, George Hartzog's task force took a fresh look, hoping that the Park Service could "play a more significant role in the exploration and development of an area which possibly has greater recreational potential than any other on the continent of North America."

Perhaps because of George Collins's own experiences, the topic of the Brooks Range in "Operation Great Land" was still the Arctic National Wildlife Range, though the report included territory as far west as Anaktuvuk Pass. The report was never made public, probably for the same reasons that caused Udall to back off from a film on park opportunities statewide in Alaska. It must have served, nevertheless, to give Hartzog some important ideas to talk about when, later that year, he conducted the secretary of the interior's Advisory Board on National Parks, Historic Sites, Buildings, and Monuments on an Alaskan tour during which Joe Fitzgerald of the Federal Field Committee talked about park possibilities. Assistant Secretary for Fish and Wildlife and Parks Stanley Cain accompanied the party, and Udall himself joined the group for several days.

Hartzog established an NPS Alaska Field Office in 1966 and in the following year gave Alaska Governor Walter Hickel a briefing book of park possibilities, referring to the Alatna–Kobuk rivers region as "qualifying as a possible addition to the National Park System." He invited Hickel to cooperate in a study of the area but received no definite reply.

The growing interest in preservation measures for the central Brooks Range caused its custodian, the Bureau of Land Management, to consider roadless-area status for the North Fork of the Koyukuk and the Alatna Basin in order to protect their wilderness value from the effects of a proposed road up the John River to the Arctic Coast oil fields. (A winter road called the Hickel Highway was punched up the valley in 1968 but was left, a sodden scar, when it was decided that the Trans-Alaska Oil Pipeline route would follow the Middle Fork of the Koyukuk farther east.) Meanwhile, the Park Service began to evaluate a number of Alaska sites under the National Landmark program, and in 1970 presented the BLM with plaques designating the Arrigetch Peaks and Walker Lake as National Natural Landmarks. Since then, thirty-seven other sites in the Brooks Range have been proposed for the National Register of Natural Landmarks.

That same year, the service decided to make an "Arctic probe" of the Alatna region under the leadership of park planner Merrill J. Mattes. As could be expected, Mattes hailed the scenery and unique ecosystem, noting that the region is not always hostile but "often mild and friendly," and one "which has been waiting, like Cinderella, for something to happen."

"What could and should happen," he wrote, "is the creation of a national park in this Arctic mountain wilderness." His team recommended a two-unit park flanking the presumed transportation corridor up the John River Valley. The park would embrace the arctic wilderness of the North Fork of the Koyukuk, dominated by Mount Doonerak and the Gates of the Arctic, and the upper Kobuk–Alatna rivers region including the Arrigetch Peaks, Mount Igikpak, and Iniakuk, Walker, and Selby lakes, among others. It was the first time that a park plan had actually been drawn upon central Brooks Range maps. It was Mattes and his team who chose the evocative name Gates of the Arctic, which seemed to move and appeal to all who heard it.

Udall realized that the 1968 discovery of oil on the North Slope could well jeopardize the freeze he had placed on Alaskan federal land disposal pending settlement of the Native land claims. As Lyndon Johnson's administration neared its close, Udall urged Johnson to make a president's "parting gift to future generations" with a package of national monument proclamations under authority of the Antiquities Act of 1906. Gates of the Arctic National Monument was to be among them. Johnson signed some proclamations but not that one. Illness, pique at a press leak, political sensitivities all have been blamed. It almost happened but not quite, but that disappointment could in retrospect be counted a blessing. In "The Fight to Save Wild Alaska," an account published in 1982 by the National Audubon Society, journalist Robert Cahn pointed out that had the whole package been proclaimed, the national-interest lands provisions might never have been included in the Alaska Native Claims Settlement Act. New Alaskan parklands might have been limited to those in the proclamation, resulting in the protection of only two additional patches of the Brooks Range.

Not that additional attempts to establish a Gates of the Arctic park were ended. Representative John Saylor introduced legislation to accomplish what the proclamation would have done, and a movement for more national parklands and wildlife preserves in Alaska was soon to build. In 1970, conservationist Richard J. Gordon delineated a larger proposal including suggestions from Robert Marshall's brother George and backed by the Alaskan Conservation Society and the Alaska chapter of the Sierra Club. It took the two proposed park units over the Arctic Divide to include Arctic Slope headwaters and several fine lakes; proposed a Utukok wildlife range in the western part of the Arctic Slope; and urged Wild River status for the Noatak, Killik, and Wind rivers, and East Fork of the Chandalar.

Then came enactment of the Alaska Native Claims Settlement Act late in 1971, with its authorization for withdrawals of land for study as possible national parks, wildlife refuges, forests, and wild and scenic rivers. The details of how that political drama was played are well recounted in Cahn's work and in G.Frank Williss's *Do Things Right the First Time: The National Park Service and the Alaska National Interest Conservation Act of 1980.* The first part of the title is from an exhortation from the newly appointed secretary of the interior, Rogers C. B. Morton, delivered when his department's senior officials first met to discuss the new act. As mentioned earlier, credit for including the national interest in the legislative provisions would seem due Joe Fitzgerald and Dave Hickock of Fitzgerald's Federal Field Committee staff. The person who put it across politically, however, seems to have been George Hartzog, working with Senator Alan Bible and other key figures in Congress.

Hartzog was under the impression that nearly all of the lands reserved in the national interest were to be for parks, and he was thinking big: conversion of the Arctic National Wildlife Range into a great park of international dimensions and a huge Gates of the Arctic National Park (which Senator Alan Bible suggested go all the way to the Arctic Ocean). Hartzog was dismayed at the eventual apportionment of the reserved lands that gave park interests only a part of what was to be studied.

The Alaska Native Claims Settlement Act of 1971 confirmed to the Native peoples of Alaska nearly 12 percent of Alaska and nearly $1 billion in cash. It also confirmed Alaska's statehood entitlement of 28 percent of the Great Land, a domain as large as California for half a million people. The rest, all but a scant one million privately owned acres, would remain federal. The most spectacular of it—the most magnificent natural features, archaeological sites, and wildlife habitats not already in national parks, forests, or refuges—would be reserved for six years, to be studied during that time for the four national systems of parks, forests, wildlife refuges, and wild and scenic rivers. In short, Congress gave a land commitment to the state and Alaska's Natives, but it only promised to *consider* protection of the most splendid parts of the Great Land.

Nevertheless, despite some overlappings and disgruntlement over who had what and over state and Native-selected tidbits that were seen as important for national protection, it seemed that each dog should be well content with its own meaty bone. If the rivalries could be settled and some adjustments in boundaries made, all should go well. Little did we then know that there would be nine years of political wrestling before the reserved lands would at last receive much-compromised protection, with Alaska fighting against it all the way.

It seemed also that Bob Marshall's dream of an unspoiled northern Alaska could come true, at least in part. All was wild except for the settlements and subsistence activities of the few, mostly Native residents. True, the area had been cleft by TAPS, the huge Trans-Alaska Pipeline System built to bring oil southward from Prudhoe Bay to Prince William Sound. Oil flowed south; "progress" poured north through the breach. But TAPS was stalled for a time by legal action brought by environmental organizations appalled at what the line might do. Even prodevelopment leaders admitted later that the delay was a blessing, as early designs for a buried pipeline would have been disastrous. The delays necessitated by the lawsuits enabled the oil consortium to do more homework on how to treat arctic regimes.

Many of us who looked at TAPS's effect upon the Brooks Range were more concerned over the haul road, built to construct the line and serve the oil fields, than over the pipeline itself, because of the overuse—and probable misuse—that the road implied. Some of us wished that an alternative proposal involving use of a railroad instead of a highway might have been chosen. We believed that it would have had far less impact on the land and its wildlife.

Completed in 1974, the narrow, shoulderless gravel haul road of steep grades and headlong truck traffic was long restricted to industrial users only, plus a few local residents and mining-claim holders along the way. In 1980, however, it was opened to public summertime use almost as far as the Continental–Arctic Divide in the heart of the Brooks Range. It was named the James Dalton Highway in honor of a member of an Alaskan pioneer family who had worked on arctic construction projects for many years.

Uncontrolled recreational use could—can—jeopardize the Brooks Range country on both sides of the pipeline road corridor. According to Dr. Steven B. Young of the Center for Northern Studies in Wolcott, Vermont, the pipeline and haul road, so often likened to mere threads across a vast landscape, could have ecological impacts for at least fifty miles on either side, and probably more as people moved ever outward. Even so, there remained vast reaches of mountain terrain on either side of the corridor where Marshall's "pioneer conditions" could be retained if the land were dedicated to wilderness and wildlife values and not left up for grabs. And if the federal land managers would effectively manage land use, access from a road could be controlled as carefully as could access by aircraft.

And virtually all of the Brooks Range *was* reserved for park and wildlife refuge purposes except for the pipeline corridor and the area now designated the National Petroleum Reserve in Alaska, under Bureau of Land Management jurisdiction.

The only notable omissions from protection were major portions of the southern foothills and flanks of the mountains with their many important glacial lakes. Parts had been selected by Native corporations (and more would be) and also by the state of Alaska because of mining potential. Settlement of a federal–state lawsuit early in the park planning process took more out of the park resources intended for federal reservation. That compromised the integrity of the south slope ecosystems for which protection was hoped for by conservationists in Alaska and nationwide. Efforts were later made to restore these lands to national status, especially by the Sierra Club, but it proved politically impossible. The Park Service called them Areas of Ecological Concern in an effort to emphasize their importance to the adjacent parks and in hope of protection through cooperative management. Moreover, a strategy-minded NPS put them on maps, making their significance a matter of official record, so that conservation organizations and Congress itself would have an official basis for adding them to protected areas. Unfortunately, they remained, for the most part, evidence only of wishful thinking.

Anemones blooming beneath a Brooks Range ledge. (National Park Service photograph by the author)

With the land east of the pipeline eyed for a major expansion of the Arctic National Wildlife Range, the Park Service's territory for study in the Brooks Range lay to the west. The service was well prepared to evaluate park potential because of the work of Richard Stenmark of the Alaska Field Office. He had served as executive secretary of an Alaska parks and monuments committee advisory to Walter Hickel, who had become secretary of the interior. Later, Stenmark assisted the Joint Federal–State Land Use Planning Commission for Alaska, which monitored and evaluated the whole Alaskan land allocation effort.

The Park Service had developed a plan by which the National Park System could more completely represent the best of America's natural and cultural heritage, and Stenmark had been thinking along similar lines in the context of Alaska. He was well prepared, therefore, when he was summoned to Washington, D.C., at the beginning of 1972 to advise on what lands Secretary Morton should reserve for parks. For the decisions that took place, conservation organizations also gave important input. A recommendation apparently first made by Alaska conservationist Walter Parker was to add the Noatak River Basin, the largest mountain-ringed river basin in arctic America with biological and hydrological integrity virtually intact. It was a choice that Francis Williamson, a science advisor from the Smithsonian Institution, pronounced to be the best choice of all of the national-interest lands reserved for study.

The Kobuk River below the Norutak Hills, Gates of the Arctic National Preserve. (National Park Service photograph by the author)

ENTERING
THE GATES

This is hallowed ground—use of it is a privilege.

—Theodor R. Swem

As a result of all the preparations that followed the Alaska Native Claims Settlement Act, our work was well marked out for us when we planners arrived in Alaska in May 1972. Immediately west of the Alaskan oil pipeline corridor the lands reserved for study included a broad, natural transection across the Arctic Divide that included the entire North Fork of the Koyukuk River and its Gates of the Arctic, as well as a north-flowing counterpart on the Arctic Slope: the Itkillik River Valley as far north as Itkillik Lake.

The best of the John River Valley to the west was also reserved, despite the scar left by the infamous Hickel Highway. The two-unit park area previously proposed could thereby be joined into one.

The Alatna Valley and Arrigetch Peaks formed the heart of the area to be studied, while to the north, across a broad plateau, a huge reach of the Arctic Slope was reserved all the way to the Colville River. This included an outstanding wild river, the Killik, matching the Alatna to form a second major band of potential parkland transecting across the range.

Ecology was an important consideration in Brooks Range park planning. Wanted were ample reaches of the arctic environment north of the divide and also of the subarctic world on the southern flanks of the range. Both places held important lakes. Kurupa and Cascade were in the north. In the south, Iniakuk lay at the threshold of the Alatna Valley, and there was Walker, already a national landmark. In a boot-shaped territory reserved amid a region gerrymandered by mining activities and hopes flowed the upper Kobuk River, fed by several other large lakes.

Farther west, beyond the Native villages of Kobuk and Ambler, the Kobuk River Valley between the Waring and Baird mountains also was marked out for park study. Initial interest there had focused on the Kobuk Sand Dunes south of the river, an anomalous glacial deposit that had created a twenty-five-square-mile subarctic Sahara. First viewing the valley and mountains as simply a context for the dunes, the park planners soon realized that they were involved with one of the greatest cultural park possibilities in North America. The Kobuk country had for thousands of years been a theater for human ecology—humanity's interactions with a life-disciplining environment. Onion Portage on the Kobuk was a renowned archaeological site, and the human ecology continued in the living communities of the valley. There amid considerable scenic splendor and wildlife richness still dwelt a hunter-gatherer society attuned to the biological rhythms of the subarctic world.

Two significant wild river valleys, those of the Salmon and the Squirrel, adjoined the Kobuk Dunes area on the west. At the reserved Cape Krusenstern area on the Chukchi Sea, where the Brooks Range dies in the Mulgrave and Igichuk hills, archaeological values predominated. There on beach ridges camped upon by early fishermen, sealers, and whalers, evidence of almost every era of Inupiat prehistory had been found. At most archaeological sites, cultural remains are piled one upon another, and archaeologists must dig down through the layers. At Krusenstern, where beach deposits built up and people moved ever westward to water's edge, the book of time lies open on the strand.

Also in the west, between the Baird Mountains and the De Long Mountains of the Arctic Divide, stretches the immensity of the Noatak Basin, some three hundred miles long and seventy-five miles wide. It is a trove of subarctic and arctic America, used by Inupiat people for ages but virtually untouched by modern human impacts. After leading a biological survey of the basin, Steven Young of the Center for Northern Studies judged that the Noatak Valley and the countryside around it "afford one of the last opportunities in the United States, or for that matter the entire world, to set aside for the future a wilderness of such size, variability, and complexity that it functions as a complete ecosystem. If this opportunity is not seized upon, it will never occur again."

Having been permanently transferred to Alaska to help plan for new parklands there, I aspired to work in the grand and glittering Wrangells in the southeast. My old friend and mentor Ted Swem, in charge of us all, knew better. He assigned me the planning of the central Brooks Range and the Noatak Basin, knowing I would therewith fall in love. Pulled from other Park Service jobs for temporary duty to help with what was considered the most urgent park planning, and lending varied expertise to the effort were my teammates: ecologist A. R. Weisbrod, landscape architect James LaRock, and interpretive planner Paul McCrary. Other planning teams studied the adjacent Kobuk Valley and Cape Krusenstern regions of the south and west where there was special emphasis on archaeology and human ecology. A veteran planner, Albert G. Henson, wisely and gently led us all as chief of the Alaska Planning Office, supporting our enthusiasms, steadying our frustrations, keeping us pulling together—forward.

With our study areas staked out for us, our first job, before beginning our proposals, was to suggest any adjustments we felt were needed to include other important areas and to see if the reservations accurately covered the existing park resources. We were to trim if we could so as to provide for any expansion of national-interest lands that might be warranted elsewhere in Alaska, and there were Native and state claims to be considered. In setting schedules, the government had no thought of the time required for field work. The secretary of the interior had to make the final reservations of land in September, and it was already June. With all the mapping and report-writing to be done, we had less than six weeks to look at the entire central and western Brooks Range and come up with recommendations.

Nearly all of our work had to be done by air, of course. We did take a couple of probing hikes to learn how the country "felt," and we used a helicopter on occasion to check out some of Bob Marshall's special wonders. The major expedition of our study season was an exploratory float trip down the Noatak River. To my knowledge, there had not been such a voyage down almost the full length of the river, at least not an official one, since Philip Smith's Geological Survey trip of 1911. We felt not far behind S. B. McLenegan's first exploration of 1885.

Ours was a joint expedition of the National Park Service, the Bureau of Sport Fisheries and Wildlife (now the U.S. Fish and Wildlife Service), and the Bureau of Outdoor Recreation, the latter having charge of studies for the National Wild and Scenic Rivers System. David Dapkus represented the Bureau of Outdoor Recreation; David Cline, a wildlife biologist, upheld his bureau's interest in the wildlife of the area. My team made up the rest of the party, together with NPS archaeologist Robert F. Nichols and glacial geologist Thomas D. Hamilton of the University of Alaska.

That the Noatak qualified as a Wild River was obvious. What we began to realize further, however, was the significance of the whole Noatak Basin as a wild reserve. The river itself was merely the central thread. We sensed, as had The Smithsonian Institution's Frank Williamson, that here might be scientific values of worldwide significance. Young was later to confirm this in his biological survey of this, the largest mountain-ringed wilderness basin in North America.

Young's survey found the Noatak to contain virtually every type of arctic habitat except for coastal formations, with perhaps the finest array of flora anywhere in the far north. Close to the region where Asia and America were once joined, the Noatak was deemed a prime location for studying a rich biota placed there by convergent influences from most of the world's mountain systems. And there was important archaeological evidence of human occupancy dating back more than ten thousand years.

"Here we're dealing with an honest-to-goodness wilderness," he commented. "There are very few of these regions left, certainly not in the United States—areas the size of a small-size eastern state. In Canada there is quite a bit left, but nowhere near as variable as this. . . . We probably have more different things around the Noatak basin than almost anywhere else of comparable size in the far north."

"We have been amazed at the variety of both large habitat and microenvironments we have been able to work with," Young continued in an interview at the close of his field investigations. "Even the basic cataloguing of the biota and major environmental situations of the Noatak region will prove to be a fertile field for scientists in many disciplines for years to come, and a great opportunity for young scientists to receive training in polar sciences under actual field conditions."

Young was concerned about how easily rare and fragile ecosystems in the area could be disturbed. "Even recreational use could result in the extinction of many species in the course of a single summer," he said, noting that the impacts of a Native settlement there two thousand years ago could still be discerned. Young also emphasized the experiential as well as the scientific importance of wilderness areas. To him, those areas were part of the basic human condition.

The whole human race evolved in wilderness, and it is part of the human psyche to be involved with and concerned with wild areas and the idea of what is over the next hill. Some will say that those days are over; that now wilderness is outer space. But going to the moon doesn't give one the feeling, say, of cresting a ridgetop in the Noatak. In going to the moon you are the final extension of a technological project. Here you have a pack on your back, alone, seeing what you can find. There's no one sitting at a computer programming what you are to be doing. I hate the thought of my grandchildren not having a chance to do what I'm doing here. We can't preserve the unknown but we can preserve the wonder and vastness and scope, so that future generations

will have some feeling of what the world in general was like and,
particularly, what the far north was like, and hopefully continues to
be like.

In checking out the reserved lands we did one thing right and one thing wrong, and we wrung our hands in sad frustration over a third event. We were right in keeping the John River Valley in the reservation, despite the Hickel Highway's scar and the impression from overflights that the valley had no noteworthy features. To split potential wild parkland into two chunks would leave them vulnerable from an intervening nonpark corridor, we realized. After all, small areas of park are more susceptible to outside influences than are large ones. When I got on the river in a canoe a year later, I was thankful that we had decided as we did. The John is not just another Brooks Range valley. It is spectacularly unique.

We made a terrible mistake in trimming out the Ambler, Shungnak, and Kogoluktuk valleys despite the advice of Dick Stenmark that they were fine parklands indeed. Acreage for reservation was needed elsewhere, and these areas did seem redundant to us. When I at last got there on the ground, I realized how wrong we had been, and I tried desperately to get those valleys back into the park proposal. I was successful with the upper Ambler, but not with the others. Mining claims there apparently daunted the Department of the Interior decision-makers. I learned later that the claims had been dropped. I was particularly sad about the Kogoluktuk. What a beautiful place!

We were devastated at the news that, in settlement of the lawsuit with Alaska over state selections on the southern flanks of the central Brooks Range, all of the lower Alatna country, Iniakuk Lake, and the best of the John River Valley were out of bounds. So were magnificent Wild Lake and Wild River, state-selected because of some old gold claims. Some of the later park bills included these areas, which were important not only as part of the regional ecosystem but also as gateway areas that needed controls integrated with park management. They never made it to park status, however. The chance that copper and other base metals might be found there kept the state and its mining-industry friends ever dreaming. Although mining the few big deposits already found was not economical, few hopes were dampened, and an access road was envisioned, running westward from what was to be named the Dalton Highway along the oil pipeline. The potential of mining became the biggest bugaboo of the early efforts to protect the central Brooks Range, especially its southern flanks.

Knowing how severe can be the impacts of mining, especially on a tender environment, environmentalists strove to contain the mining in already identified sites outside recommended park areas. They disbelieved any claims of economic advantage from such remote deposits, pointing to closed mines in other, accessible regions of the nation. As for the consequences of letting miners loose in the Brooks Range, they pointed to a major copper claim known as Arctic in the Shungnak River watershed. There an airstrip had been built and heavy equipment brought in to carve out a network of roads and test-drilling sites to find and map the ore deposit precisely. The ridge looked as if a war had been fought there, and it came to be regarded by many as a classic example of what not to do in the Brooks Range.

Geologists, however, had identified a mineralized belt running across the south-central Brooks Range. Drawn on maps with a broad brush, it was hailed by Alaskan mining interests as denoting a region loaded with potential wealth and not to be "locked up" in parks closed to mining. Actually, although the geology was considered generally favorable for occasional base-metal occurrences, geologists admitted that the chances of finding deposits of minable quality and quantity would be extremely rare: out of hundreds of mineral occurrences, only a score might be worth $100,000. Two or three might be worth $1 million. One might make a paying mine, all expenses considered. They would also be small in area. I understand that the Arctic deposit itself involves only 120 acres. In the west, the Red Dog discovery, a base-metals deposit on the western edge of the Noatak Basin hailed as world class, is reportedly only a single square mile in extent.

Nevertheless, the exploration of one proven deposit had been so devastating that we park planners shuddered at the impact if more were discovered. In fairness to the mining companies, it must be said that they quickly learned to be gentler with their Earth probings, and often used helicopter-borne drill rigs to test the rocks. Yet no matter how confined and gentle the mining might be, it would wound much of the Brooks Range's environment, we feared, not only with mines themselves but also with support facilities—mining camps and transportation systems. Mining of existing valid claims has not proliferated in the Brooks Range beyond a few long-known deposits, but dreams of copper, lead, and zinc, and even revived visions of a bit of gold, deprived much important country of permanent protection.

Secretary of the Interior Rogers Morton made his final land reservations in September 1972. Then we got down to work on specific proposals for the Gates of the Arctic region and for the Noatak, developing concepts that had been forming in the course of looking at those extraordinary land resources. Other park planners tackled the Kobuk and Cape Krusenstern areas.

We were asked repeatedly why so much land was needed for a park. There is redundancy in the Brooks Range's vast succession of ridges and valleys, commenters advised; confine park protection to a few "museum exhibits"—especially spectacular areas like the Arrigetch Peaks—and leave the rest of the land open to other uses, like mining.

We soon realized, however, that the most critical resource was size, spaciousness itself. Steve Young's words about the Noatak were applicable to the whole arctic region. Where animals must forage so far, where all life is stretched so thin, protections must come broadly.

And it was important to preserve as much as possible for people themselves. With awe and dread, we realized that this was America's last big chunk of raw wilderness, the last land of solitude. There would never be any more. For more than three hundred years, Americans had always been able to count on a frontier, and a wilderness hinterland. Always there was a place to "go and look behind the ranges," as the British writer Rudyard Kipling put it. This was the ultimate range, and already it had been looked behind by the oil men. Together with some other Alaskan fastnesses and a few shreds and patches elsewhere in the country, the Brooks Range was all that was left of once wild America.

Ever in mind was Bob Marshall's observation that "in Alaska alone can the emotional values of the frontier be preserved," and his exhortation that "in the name of a balanced use of American resources, let's keep northern Alaska largely a wilderness!" Somehow, the nation would have to make this last remnant do, forever, what the whole American wilderness had done to challenge and mold and temper and inspire us as a people and nation. To make the quality last would require all the area that could possibly be set aside. So easy to damage and so slow to heal is the northern environment that human use must be spread as thinly and lightly as possible. So gaunt and open is the landscape, moreover, that it is hard to know solitude if other people are abroad. Endless nooks and crannies of geography would be required if many people were to have a sense of exploration and discovery. Here was a land for experiences, not merely sights to see.

As for recommendations for "developing" a park, our obvious and immediate decision was right out of Marshall's book: Do absolutely nothing. Draw a protective boundary and leave the place alone: no roads, no trails, no bridges, no campgrounds, no interpretive signs, none of the woodsy aids and conveniences with which most parks are equipped. They would change the character and quality of the land. As Roger Allin had recommended, visitors would take the Brooks Range on *its* terms, not theirs. Without the trappings that engender arrogance, they might gain refreshment from humility and awe, and the wilderness would endure.

If there were to be a very few scattered patrol cabins, let them be of logs in the timbered lands and of sod like igloos of the tundra. Later, we doubted even the wisdom of this, feeling that the managers should be as nomadic and light of impact as their visiting wards. Although abjuring the extremists' suggestions that the Brooks Range be a don't-expect-to-be-rescued wilderness, we borrowed a karate term to call it a black-belt park. Not for neophytes, it would be at the ascetic end of a spectrum of national parks in Alaska that would range from the comforts of hotels and cruise ships to the most basic of wilderness survival. The Alaskan park system seemed one to be most appropriately regarded as a balanced totality, with no one park needing to be all things to all people.

We saw difficulty of access as a value, not a problem. Actually, the Brooks Range is far more traversable than, say, the gigantic topography of the Wrangells or the perpendicular tangles of southeastern Alaska and parts of the Alaskan Peninsula. As Merrill Mattes had noted, it is often mild and "friendly" in summer. Yet the weather is far too fickle, the land too severe, the distances too remote to be encountered casually or ill prepared. And it has its own mystique. All shuddered to think of a time when there might be guidebooks, features-to-see publications, for if one knows what is there, a wilderness experience becomes just a sightseeing trip. We remembered Aldo Leopold's comment in his landmark book *A Sand County Almanac*, "I am glad I shall never be young without wild country to be young in. Of what avail are forty freedoms without a blank spot on the map?"

Also to remember was the time warp on which the planning must be woven. Our planning was not just for the here and now. It must be proof against short-range economic convenience, appetite. We felt charged with setting up a great land trust, its assets to be counted biologically. We had to try to look hundreds of years into the future, down the generations when the great-great-grandchildren of present-day Americans would need a wilderness dimension to life. There would have to be safekeepings of biotic integrity, places of rich spiritual content, where roots could be felt and heavens heard.

Although wilderness preservation is a humanistic as well as a biological consideration, we recognized that its value to human beings is not a matter to be weighed in use statistics. It is a matter of quality. A single person's awareness, understanding, and concern deepened through wilderness involvement may be of more help and benefit to us in our Earth care than the machine-derived pleasure of thousands.

We wanted to obliterate climbers' summit cairns and other such petty little human monuments that destroy another's sense of discovery with a boastful "I was here first." We hoped there would be no more geographic naming, convinced that it means more to essay a nameless summit or valley than one tamed by nomenclature. Concerned about the low productivity of arctic fishes, we suggested no more killing of fish than camp fare might require.

Our one great concession to modernity caused concern to all who felt deeply about the value of wilderness per se, above and beyond human enjoyments. That criticizable concession was access by air, an already established fact of life by the time of the studies. We had misgivings about it but realized how difficult, politically, it would be to establish a walk-in park so large that a pedestrian would need more weeks to get into it than he or she could expect to have free. As Roderick Nash, author of *Wilderness and the American Mind,* was to point out later in a special report on Brooks Range air access, the airplane has been to Alaska what the horse was to the American West. Moreover, air travel does not bring on the impact that roads do.

The key was control; indeed, to determine how much use the park could support, what types of use, and where. Accessibility invites degradation. If a finite area, no matter how big, is to be relied upon for centuries to provide a certain kind of experience, it must not ever be overused or abused, or it will soon be used up, worn into a shabby shadow of its former self and former value. One can well liken a Brooks Range experience to seeing a world-championship athletic event or hearing a world-famous musician. What matter the planning and waiting if the experience is worth it, and not merely a semblance, battered and faded and debased, casually got and therefore casually valued?

None who had studied Alaska's recreation resources seem to have considered such need for controls, or at least to have discussed it. Marshall came close, but he may not have foreseen fully what air travel might do to his wilderness.

His brother George did as time passed, and more and more aircraft came north. He wrote that Bob would have been "outraged" had his "splendid wilderness solitude" been shattered by the landing of an airplane. "If there is to be any full wilderness left, it will be necessary to zone areas where aircraft may and where they may not land," George Marshall wrote.

Collins talked glowingly about recreation but not about limits. Territorial Governor B. Frank Heintzleman, in his foreword to the Alaska Recreation Survey Report of 1955, spoke of the economic benefits of "recreational wares" and of making them "more accessible and their use more enjoyable and safe." Allin recognized that, when wilderness resources elsewhere in America had eroded, the pressure would be upon those in Alaska. He may have foretold our ponderings when he wrote, "It is expected that as these pressures develop, so will our plan evolve." But then he added, "as will our contribution to the proper development of Alaska's natural resources." (We assumed that he meant development in other, more appropriate places in Alaska, not in his and our beloved Brooks.)

"Operation Great Land" observed that in most frontier regions wilderness is not taken seriously as a resource, and we planners of it worried lest private exploitation ruin it for short-term profit through "helter-skelter unplanned developments." But the report added, "What it has must be known and made available while still maintaining its integrity."

This was echoed in George Hartzog's "Deskbook" of park possibilities for Governor Hickel: "Future development—by air, land, and water—would undoubtedly attract many visitors to the scenic wonders of this subarctic wilderness."

To Merrill Mattes, the enemy of Alaska's pristine glory was private exploitation. A public park was different, and he envisioned an eventual arctic one with all the trimmings, acknowledging that "it might be some years before the full management, protection and interpretation of such a park could be implemented and visitors could be accommodated."

What all these trains of thought reflected was the National Park Service mission as spelled out in the act of Congress that established it in 1916, a time when parks were often referred to as "pleasuring grounds": "To conserve the scenery and the natural and historic objects and the wildlife therein and to provide for the enjoyment of the same in such manner and by such means as will leave them unimpaired for the enjoyment of future generations."

It was a paradoxical dual ideal of preservation with use, wherein use was politically the more powerful by far. And to anyone to whom the term *conservation* might mean "to consume carefully and to make last as long as possible," whatever was being conserved would, at some point, be used up or at least degraded. For National Park Service planners, preservation with use was an ideological inheritance of our profession at a time when there was much talk about recreational demand—politically imperious demand. Yet here were resources, fragile and finite, physical but also experiential, dependent upon our devising a management strategy that would allow them to endure forever, forever in finest quality, offering discovery and solitude no matter how many people might seek recreation in the Great Land. It was, in a way, a wilderness trust fund, capable of yielding unforgettable dividends only if the capital were not invaded.

Moreover, as Edward Abbey was to suggest in one of his essays in *Down the River*, published in 1982, perhaps some of the wilderness should exist in its own right, for its own sake. It might be called "an absolute wilderness," he wrote, "justified by our recognition of the rights of other living things to a place of their own, an evolution of their own not influenced by human pressure."

To keep the "capital" of the Brooks Range pristinely intact over long time, we recommended a device that was to become the cornerstone of all our planning:

a reservation and permit system. Free and without favor, computerized to make a Brooks Range booking as easy as making an airline or hotel reservation, it could keep precise control of the numbers of people in the region and how they were deployed throughout it to give them solitude and spread their impact to keep the area below the threshold of wear.

"Hello, Gates of the Arctic National Park? Three friends and I would like to hike in the upper North Fork Koyukuk country during the first two weeks of August."

"That's fine, your name, please? Consider that area reserved for you. Give us a travel plan as soon as possible." Or "We're sorry to say that the upper North Fork is already reserved for that time, but if you can move your trip two weeks either way, we'll be happy to reserve it for you." Or "The upper North Fork is already spoken for during all of August, but if you'll consider changing your destination to the headwaters of Clear River, not far away, it's available to you any time during that month. We can either mail you your permits or you can pick them up in Anchorage, Fairbanks, or Bettles."

So it might go, each group to its own valley, lake, or mountain summit, with river trips scheduled so that one party did not impinge on another. Air travel into the park would be coordinated with the reservations on the basis of one trip in, one trip out, and air drops of food as necessary. No hopping about by air and intruding on other people's reserved areas.

In such a system, we foresaw many advantages to park visitors. You could count on an experience of the highest quality, of the solitude and sense of discovery that wilderness alone can provide—a very private experience with no other tents in sight, no other group of backpackers coming over the hill to your little mountain lake, or canoes and rafts floating round the bend and heading in to pitch their tents beside yours. No danger of planning a trip for months and years, paying the air fare, backpacking into the mountains for days, and finally reaching a long-anticipated destination deep in the wilderness only to find the Sierra Club or a Boy Scout troop already there in force, or sportsmen with a case of beer and a tape deck flown in for the day from a commercial lodge.

And the system would have a highly important safety factor. In case of trouble—injury on the trip, or tragedy at home—the Park Service would know where you were, where to find you.

For the park managers, the system would be equally beneficial. No erosive overuse of favored areas would occur. Visitors would be dispersed—guided by permit to areas that could accept their use without degradation. Better visitor safety would result from park rangers' knowing where people were and being able to check for trouble in discreet overflights. A reservation and permit system would also prevent abuses to the park. Giving the permit would provide park personnel an opportunity to make personal contact with visitors, ensuring that they were properly equipped and knowledgeable about what they were going to do and how they should treat the park. And if there were malefactions, the park staff would know who was responsible.

The permits would be issued to visitors, not to commercial outfitters, so that the economic temptation for recreation entrepreneurs to get more and more clients into the park would be removed.

But how many people would be enough for a given area? How many would be too much? Only experience and scientific research could answer those questions. The National Park Service cannot manage what it does not understand; therefore, a strong program of basic research and monitoring of both resources and visitor experiences was called for. When trampled vegetation, trail formation, water-quality deterioration, or other signs of wear and tear began to show up, it would be time to cut back or close down an area for the long period it would need to recover. If visitors began complaining of being intruded upon by others, allocations would be altered.

Without sure knowledge at the outset of what either the biological or psychological carrying capacity of the park might be in terms of perpetuating its character and quality, the only way to begin was with conservative best judgment, using estimates of appropriate use levels that we felt were certainly below the threshold of degradation. If we erred on the cautious side, it would be far easier to increase the user quotas than to be overliberal in our estimates and disappoint people by having to cut back. Once a use level becomes established and is expected, reducing it for whatever reason is certain to be unpopular.

We were, therefore, extremely cautious in establishing recommended use levels for the proposed parkland. In this small valley, perhaps two people at a time, maybe four. Two at that small mountain tarn; four or possibly six in this headwaters area. How many groups on the bigger lakes? It might depend on whether or not they were beginning or ending a trip or just remaining. Fixed locations for park sojourns could quickly become seriously impacted. Small groups would need to be the rule. Large parties are particularly hard on resources.

Especially difficult would be maintaining a high quality of personal experience. It is far easier for a botanist to calculate damage to vegetation than for a psychologist/sociologist to gauge expectation and satisfaction. As the quality and quantity of wilderness resources have declined in America, we have become content with ever settling for less. New generations of wilderness seekers accept as satisfactory conditions that would have disappointed, even outraged, an earlier generation of outdoors people. Those with high standards move on, if they can, or die out, and a new clientele comes along to enjoy what is left, not knowing what it missed. The poorer experiences are good enough for the times, so there is little remonstrance. "You should have been here fifty years ago," they hear, and they shrug, not comprehending the lost legacy.

For the Brooks Range we were determined not to let such loss occur. Our plan was to keep intact the wilderness park resources presented to us for planning. Our hope was that visitors a century hence would find the same qualities, have the same experiences that thrilled and humbled us, walking in Bob Marshall's footsteps. We were to face serious criticism of our reservation/permit system as antithetical to the whole concept of "freedom of the wilderness." Such freedom, we were told, does not tolerate a bureaucratic system of permits. Whim and impulse are part of the wilderness experience, of wilderness enjoyment. Our reply was simply, sadly, that the world has bred itself out of the luxury of going in that good old free-roving way. Not so long ago there were comparatively few of us and plenty of good places to seek out at our leisure. Now we cannot just say, "Hey, let's go to the ball game," or "Let's see the new hit show." We must plan ahead, wait our turn, or expect standing-room-only quality at best.

I shall not here recount all the various permutations through which the conservation proposals for the central and western Brooks Range passed during eight years of study and debate. They are discussed in Frank Williss' administrative history. There were a number of different management recommendations put forth by government agencies, by the state and its congressional staffs, by conservation organizations, and one even by the Nunamiut of Anaktuvuk Pass. This last one bears comment, however, because of our positive working relationship with the Native people of the area, particularly the Nunamiut. With subsistence hunting and gathering guaranteed under the Alaska Native Claims Settlement Act, they saw park protection of wilderness conditions as in their interest, so long as use was managed so as not to interfere with their own lives. They suggested that they throw their large land selections in with much of the federal selections and create a huge cultural park they would manage jointly with the National Park Service. They would call it the Nunamiut National Wildlands. At one point this concept was officially espoused, with the name Koyukon added to involve the Athapaskans to the south. The preserve would be flanked by a two-unit Gates of the Arctic National Wilderness Park. Retention of wilderness conditions, for the local people or for visitors, was the underlying management principle. This proposal was one of many that ultimately were rejected or modified.

For the huge Noatak Basin farther west our governing principle was scientific research in a wilderness context. Here was a resource of international significance, where studies of living, changing plant and animal systems, how they relate to each other, and how man's activities affect and are affected by them can be studied and managed. The basin would be a reservoir for preserving wild plants and animals to assure that the genetic material there would not be lost, a place where the environmental scientists of the world could be drawn together to address problems of concern to all of us.

Under this concept, the whole wilderness region drained by a Noatak Wild River would be under the administration of the Park Service and Bureau of Sport Fisheries and Wildlife in partnership. The former would have charge of overall administration, including what recreational use was appropriate. The latter would manage the wildlife.

The real managers in our thinking, however, would be a board of top-ranking scientists who would advise the secretary of the interior on how the Noatak reserve was to be run. The principal purpose of the protection was for research, both baseline and experimental, and only such recreational use would be permitted as the scientists agreed was neither erosive nor in conflict with the research, and was otherwise appropriate.

Although the board of scientist advisors technically would have no administrative authority, that being by law vested in the secretary, we envisioned that it would be so prestigious a body that no manager would flout its recommendations. Although we later found that the Noatak Basin has some fine hiking country, we did not think at the time that it would be as attractive to wilderness recreationists as the regions of higher mountains farther east. The river use, we felt sure, could be easily regulated in the interest both of scientific objectives and wilderness experience. The wilderness mystique of the Noatak was so strong as to make the river a place where absolute solitude was essential. The footprints encountered on its shores should be those of wild animals.

As the Noatak did not quite seem to fit the national park mold, at least compared with the adjacent Gates of the Arctic area, already targeted for park status, we suggested that the jointly managed area be called Noatak National Ecological Reserve. The name later became even more of a mouthful—Arctic Valleys National Ecological Reserve—when, for a time, it included the drainage of the Squirrel River, which was also studied for National Wild River status. Later, for a time, the Noatak was proposed as a National Range under the joint management of the Bureau of Land Management and the Bureau of Sport Fisheries and Wildlife.

Limestack Mountain looms above Greylime Creek near Ernie Pass. (National Park Service photograph by the author)

Eventually, the Noatak Basin was established as a National Preserve, the Park Service in charge. Although authorized by law, the idea of advisory guidance by a board of scientists faded. In 1974, however, the Noatak Basin had been designated a World Biosphere Reserve by the United Nations Educational, Scientific and Cultural Organization. Moreover, the Arctic Research and Policy Act of 1984 gave new impetus to much-needed arctic research in America. Scientists everywhere will doubtless be watching the Noatak.

These were the philosophical foundations upon which we built our conservation proposals. Addressing a largely predetermined territory to plan wilderness parks with carefully controlled use would seem an easy task, but politics would not have it so. Our concerns that proposal boundaries were flawed, not containing entire ecosystems, were such that we tugged at the mining interests and tried to beg loose from state or Native selection some lands strategic to our needs but marginal to theirs. I have mentioned efforts to get the upper Ambler, Shungnak, and

Kogoluktuk drainages back into the national park proposal. A mining claim slopped needlessly over the rim of the Reed River drainage. The best of the John River Valley had been lost to the park because evidence of copper had been reported there. The Killik was claimed as Nunamiut homeland, though a recreational easement down it was granted later. Lovely Lake Minakokosa protruded entirely from the park into state territory, and other key lakes like Iniakuk and Wild on the south and Kurupa and Cascade on the north were out altogether.

The nature of subsistence rights was an issue of vast complexity. So was sport hunting. The sportsmen were resentful that Native subsistence hunting, under controversial definition, could continue although the sportsmen would be shut out from large areas. Strong opposition to the Alaskan park proposals was coming from hunters, both in Alaska and nationwide, who saw their opportunities shrinking and did not want huntable lands closed to them. Secretary of the Interior Morton therefore began considering whether or not national parks with hunting allowed might be a feasible solution peculiar to Alaska. Classic park tradition was against it. Parks were wildlife sanctuaries (except for the hapless fish).

But the Alaskan parks were to be huge wildernesses, use would be light, and hunting was a strong element of Alaskan culture. Hunting was mankind's original way of experiencing wilderness, and there was much philosophical literature on the value of hunting in sharpening a human being's awareness of natural regimes. Moreover, Alaska had a respected coterie of professional guides and other hunters who followed the precepts of "fair-chase" hunting: no quickie fly-ins, no mechanical contrivances and conveniences to ensure success. A hunt was to be a wilderness experience of at least ten days. Hunting was afoot, with no airplanes for eyes, no radio-directed tactics. The alert search for a quarry, said the hunter-philosophers, attunes one to the wilderness in all its moods and details to an extent that no nature guide, sketch pad, or camera can match. The Brooks Range was becoming increasingly prized as a hunting ground, particularly for the Dall sheep, that pure white bighorn of the northern mountains. Close the central range, and much of the sheep hunting would be gone.

Should not the Park Service have some firsthand experience at fair-chase hunting? Many Park Service men are avid hunters, of course, though they follow the canon that there should be places where wildlife is only observed. Thinking again of that probing congressional questioning, I felt we should speak from fresh, on-the-ground experience. So, with NPS approbation, I took leave and went hunting. I fulfilled a long-standing promise to a hunter nephew by inviting him to accompany me, and for our guide I chose a young Bettles friend, John Hankee, whose professional abilities and philosophy I respected.

The choice was excellent. The temporary tent-frame camp that John and assistant guide Steve Bergeron had set up was as impeccable as were their hunting skills and ethics. My nephew Godfrey and I each got our ram, mine sighted after sixty miles of walking. Our hunting folded us as closely into our environment as I have ever been. After the effort and suspense and adrenaline of the final stalk, the kill seemed a sacrament I was sharing with hunters over half a million years. Although it had not the importance of the overall experience that it had brought about, it was the fitting culmination, the essential reason for it all.

Fair-chase hunting was indeed a valid way toward awareness and appreciation of wilderness, I reported. But not a valid concept for parks, even in Alaska, it was decided. I agreed. The hunting ethics of our times do not measure up to such a privilege. Moreover, ever since the national park idea was born with the establishment of the world's first national park, Yellowstone, in 1872, parks have been wildlife preserves. Parks people worldwide, even in Alaska, were concerned over the possibility of a big Alaskan exception to the rule. Call the areas something else if there was to be hunting, they advised, although the stature of areas like Gates of the Arctic merited that special rank that the title "Park" best denotes.

National preserves, units of the National Park System with preeminent natural values, yet where hunting can be permitted, had recently been created by Congress, and certain Alaskan areas were so designated. The Noatak was one, and the Arctic National Wildlife Refuge was also open to sport hunting, so that nearly two-thirds of the Alaskan Brooks Range was to remain huntable, for sport as well as for subsistence hunters. The latter, of course, could rely on all the land. Two portions of Gates of the Arctic, the northeastern corner and the upper Kobuk River region, were given a national preserve status, for hunting and to make a possible westward transportation corridor less destructive to the park concept. We had tried to apply the preserve approach to a larger area, but found it impossible to make any logical division of the Brooks Range into park and preserve units.

One of the most vexatious aspects of our planning was the government's and politicians' preoccupation with acreage. It seemed as if we planners were forever counting acres—how many added here, or subtracted there. It had all started with the Alaska Statehood and Native Claims Settlement acts, which contained acreage allocations. Now we were stuck with endless acre totalings. As if it made a difference! The important point was whether or not key features—watersheds, for example—

139

were included in protected areas. That a particular valley might comprise a hundred thousand acres or three hundred thousand was immaterial. We were dealing in resources, not acres, which were irrelevant to our work. In a region two hundred miles long and one hundred miles deep, millions of acres were about as comprehensible as billions of dollars in the national budget.

And because they were dealing in acres, not true geography, the mapmakers in Washington, D.C., marked out the reservations in terms of surveyors' townships six miles square and described by the township and range lines drawn on the Geological Survey maps of Alaska. Conservation proposals could be easily delineated down to about a quarter of a township. Configurations smaller than that caused the mapmaker to worry about accuracy. They were using maps on which an inch equaled four miles. To be sure, therefore, that an entire watershed, divide, or other feature was entirely inside a boundary, more land than necessary had to be included to block it in. We wanted to draw boundaries precisely where we felt they should be—usually along mountain ridges. Only out on the flat expanses of the Arctic Slope did surveyed lines become useful.

The mapmakers were resistant to natural boundaries not only because they made it hard to count acres accurately, but also because the mappers were concerned about eventual surveying. Someday someone might have to describe the boundaries by distances and bearings, and it is much easier to describe a straight section line than a mountain divide. But why, we asked, would such a survey ever be necessary? The top of the ridge was the top of the ridge, and by that travelers would know when they were inside or outside a park. In the west—the Kobuk and Noatak areas—natural boundaries were, in fact, much used. We were able to bring the eastern boundary down to the first height of land above the oil pipeline, changing the boundary from meaningless township lines. This might have suggested to the boundary-makers that they could do the same sensible thing for the western edges of the park. Elsewhere, however, where state or Native lands abutted the federal reserves, the township-line approach prevailed.

A far more serious problem was one of private inholdings. There were some ten thousand acres of such allotments strewn throughout the central and western Brooks Range, most of them located at such strategic places as river confluences and key lakes. In terms of acreage they were minuscule, but any use of them adverse to the purposes of the park could be devastating to its wilderness integrity. These private lands included five-acre headquarters sites and twenty-acre trade and manufacturing sites patented under the public land laws, and mining claims, which, if proved up, could become private property. Private lands commanded the Arrigetch Creek area in the Alatna Valley as well as Walker Lake.

Other, more ubiquitous manifestations of private ownership were Native allotments. These had been allocated to Native applicants as fishing and trapping sites and could total 160 acres per individual in as many as four parcels. They could only be sold with permission of the secretary of the interior, but that restriction was to protect the owners from being euchred by speculators, rather than to ensure that the lands stayed in subsistence use.

Planners hoped and had to assume that these private lands would eventually be bought out to consolidate resource management under one policy. Otherwise, they would remain as potential threats to the integrity of the wilderness reserves. We hoped, too, that the federal government would be generous in the buying in order to avoid the resentment landowners often feel when government presses hard-bargain buyouts. Better politically to let them go whistling to the bank.

The longer the delay, the higher the cost to taxpayers of these unique properties likely to be sought as recreational hideaways or commercial plums but likely also to be sores of development festering in a wilderness otherwise whole and clean.

Mount Igikpak and Noatak River headwaters. (National Park Service photograph by the author)

DEEP
WITHIN

*If we screw it up here . . . we can all stop
arguing, because there won't be anything left
to argue about!*

—G. Ray Bane

Noatak, I have been told by Inupiat people, means "deep inside," "from
deep within," an apt name for a great river flowing out from the heart of the
mountains from sources cupped in the cirques of Mount Igikpak. With the
planning philosophy for the proposed parklands there established, it was important
to go deep inside, and learn as much as possible about the western and central Brooks
Range. The Congress had to have confidence that the National Park Service knew
what it was talking about when it recommended a territory for park status, especially
a major area over which there was controversy. It is most unwise to urge special
reservation for land the values of which are sincerely surmised but minimally
reconnoitered. To the question "Why is it important?" congressmen want reliable
answers based on experience. Getting those answers, in as concrete terms as possible,
was the next task. With the conservation proposals outlined and conceptualized,
and with my planning team gone home, my job could have been described in the
classic traveling salesman's dictum: "You gotta know the territory."

The proposals would be criticized first of all for the size being asked for:
"Why the need for so much land? One valley is like the next." We heard such
comments from officials looking down from their airplanes during reconnaissance
tours. We were convinced of the importance of size, however, for people as well as
for wildlife. The nation's last chance for a wilderness preserve of heroic proportions
was no time for niggardly planning. The best defense against ignorant excision of
territory was firsthand experience as to what was there, and what it might mean. I
had only one field season before the first legislation was introduced at the end of

143

1973, but the process would continue for five more years as competing proposals were put forth, and the political forces wrestled.

The Bureau of Outdoor Recreation (BOR) wild river investigations greatly helped my getting to know the territory, valley by valley. I was usually the Park Service's representative in the studies of central Brooks Range rivers. As such I went down the Killik with Jules Tileston, who headed the BOR office in Alaska and had been involved with the National Wild and Scenic Rivers System since its inception; down the Tinayguk and North Fork of the Koyukuk, the John, and the Salmon, with Patrick Pourchot (later to become an Alaska state senator); and the Nigu-Etivluk with David Dapkus, who had been BOR's representative on my Noatak expedition. Later, I had the opportunity to hike in the De Long Mountains with BOR's James Morris on a wilderness study.

In addition to the official wild river study trips, I had a chance to float most of the Kobuk River, much of the Alatna, and the Wild. The upper Kobuk and the big lakes north of it—Selby-Narvak and Minakokosa—had been a bone of contention in the d-2 land withdrawal process. Alaska and the mining interests wanted that area out of the national-interest land reservation because it crossed a suggested transportation route to major mineral claims north and west. Assistant Secretary of the Interior Nathaniel P. Reed had insisted on its importance to the park proposal, and, so far, his views had prevailed. Nevertheless, pressure continued to eliminate this boot, as it was called, dangling from the main park territory as if asking to be pulled off. Our planning team had visited the lakes and knew that they were indeed gems, but was the Kobuk really worth fighting for? My friend Bob Waldrop and I took his double foldboat and found out. What a river! Magnificent, and different from the rest. It stayed in the proposal, not only for the National Wild and Scenic Rivers System but also as the core of a national preserve, though it ended up without Wilderness status because of its transportation-corridor possibilities.

Bob and I also accompanied Environmental Protection Agency Director Russell E. Train down much of the Alatna, ending with a hike to Helpmejack Lake. After passing the Arrigetch Peaks area and exploring Takahula Lake and its exquisite satellite ponds, we floated into controversial territory that had been relinquished to the state. We wanted it back, as it was not only ecologically complementary to the main Alatna Valley and environs but also included one of the major lakes in the region, Iniakuk, and much else of importance. Some of the bills in Congress were, indeed, including it in the proposed park. We never got it back, alas, for there just might be a mineral deposit somewhere about.

The same was true of Wild River and Wild Lake, left out of the reservation because of old gold claims and other state interests, and already the target of real estate development. Wild Lake is probably the most spectacular of the large lakes in the region and, like Iniakuk, an ideal starting place for wilderness traveling. As I learned firsthand, Wild River is a delightful stream, lively all the way to its confluence with the North Fork of the Koyukuk. Partway down, Gilroy Mountain forms a symbolic visual arctic gatepost, visible from the village and airfield of Bettles, the starting place for most trips into the central Brooks Range. Extending parkland down the Wild was not in the cards, however.

Running rivers was a good way of getting to know the territory, but it was far from enough. It was time to take a leaf from Robert Marshall's (and the geologists') book and start walking. After all, that was how most of the Brooks Range wilderness was to be traveled. Seeing the park resources as a pedestrian was important, not only to appraise their importance in detail but also to experience the problems and the rewards of Brooks Range wanderings. It was well that a good sampling of this way of going be accomplished by a middle-aged nonathlete, for there were constant grumblings that the proposed Alaskan parks, particularly Gates of the Arctic, would be only for the young and hardy.

What better place to start walking than through the country that Bob Marshall had extolled? Had his euphoria been justified? We should see, not merely in a few random helicopter landings, but by living in the wilderness as he had. The problems of mounting government expeditions into backcountry, both financial and logistical, were well solved by two factors: Bob Waldrop, who had worked for the Park Service off and on, was primarily a professional wilderness guide. He could save us much time and money by arranging and leading trips.

He needed clients besides me, however, and I needed other personalities to react to the experience. Fortunately, two college-age godsons of mine had come into the country: Kip Dalley, to work at what was then Mount McKinley National Park, and George Hamilton, heart-set on Alaska's wilderness. Friends came with them; friends followed them, part of a tide of ebullient, outdoors-competent young men and women attracted to Alaska in those exciting years for anyone interested in protecting some of the last frontier. My home in Anchorage became headquarters for an able gang eager to be recruited as expeditionary troops, not only in my areas of responsibility but others as well. They offered outdoor skills, some of which were highly technical and sophisticated, and academic degrees or fields of college study very helpful to our endeavors. Some became temporary government employees. Others volunteered their help for the price of an airplane ride and food. Still others, after jobbing around Anchorage and elsewhere, pooled their savings to launch private investigations often tailored to my planning needs: to find a back door to the Arrigetch country, for example, or to get behind Cockedhat Mountain to the Arctic Slope. Faithfully they reported back to augment my own personal knowledge of what the central Brooks Range was all about.

That first three-week walk with Waldrop took us from Anaktuvuk Pass over Ernie Pass, down past the Valley of the Precipices to the Gates of the Arctic, and then up the North Fork of the Koyukuk past Mount Doonerak to the Arctic Divide. Suffice it to say here that Marshall's passion was justified. Waldrop, assisted by George Hamilton, led a group of us on a more ambitious trip the following year: a walk around Mount Igikpak, highest peak in the central Brooks and in the very heart of the proposed park. Dick Stenmark, who had become a staff member of the Joint Federal-State Land Use Planning Commission for Alaska, joined the trip for some firsthand impressions.

Igikpak is a legendary peak. The Inupiat name simply means Big Mountain, I was told. Another translation is "two big peaks." To the people of the Kobuk Valley, however, it was Papiok—Fish's Tail—a name since transferred to a lesser tail-shaped peak in the upper Noatak area. At Walker Lake, a mythic trout of immense size had swallowed a child. The mother in revenge dropped hot rocks into the lake until the scalded trout leaped out, high onto the mountain. There it froze, tail up, into the twin granite spires of Igikpak's summit.

Whatever happened, it is a magical mountain, godly. It has been climbed, of course, "conquered," but I wish it had not been, not ever. It deserves approach only in reverence and awe, but how to approach it? That needed to be checked out. I should not have wanted the secretary of the interior to have to answer a congressional committee by saying, "We don't know. Our people haven't been there." His people did go there, and Igikpak is indeed the apogee of a national park. It is accessible from that national landmark, Walker Lake, as well as from the Alatna and Kobuk valleys, and thus there are appropriate wilderness ways of coming to pay homage to that majestic mountain.

Our circumambulation of Mount Igikpak had another important mission: to establish the importance of the Reed River, not only as a route to the park's heartland around Igikpak but also as a feature of significance in its own right. A major base-metal discovery lay just over the watershed, and state land selections in the interests of mining disregarded topography and, going by township and range lines, had bitten right into the Reed Valley.

Was it worth fighting for? Yes, it was, unquestionably. Reed Hot Springs, visited by Ensign M. L. Reed of the Stoney expedition in 1886, was only a minor feature, though its welling forth created an amazing lushness of vegetation. The major significance of the Reed was the stately and exquisite beauty of its course and riverscape. We all hoped that some accommodation with the mining interests might be worked out that would retain the valley's integrity.

By canoe and afoot, the National Park Service probed the heartlands of the central Brooks Range, but there was still much to do in the east, the west, and the north. The eastern edge of the area reserved for a park paralleled the Trans-Alaska Oil Pipeline corridor, but this boundary was an arbitrary line, drawn on the paper grids of townships and ranges. Between it and the pipeline was considerable territory that should be under park protection and control, we realized. The logical boundary for a park was one that could run along easily identifiable ridges immediately west of the pipeline and its road. Where exactly should such a logical boundary go? Where might people seek entrance to the park from the road if it were to be opened to public travel? With the help of Dave Mahalic of the Bureau of Land Management and of Joe Standart and Bill Resor, NPS seasonal employees, I probed eastern gateways to the park area, walking the passes and checking the valley of the Hammond River. Later, my wilderness-wise associate Ray Bane and I made the same kind of investigation farther north. Along the pipeline, our efforts to have park boundaries follow topographical features miraculously paid off, for once. We drew a boundary line on the first ridges west of the haul road, and there it stayed.

Ray and I had by then become an effective team in probing the central Brooks Range and tempering a wilderness philosophy for it. Living in Hughes and then Bettles, trained in anthropology, professionally seasoned as an arctic schoolteacher, with wilderness skills as a dog musher and hiker excelled by few, Ray and his beloved team-mate/wife, Barbara, had been closely following and supporting the conservation efforts for the north. Having loved the north and its people, having heard for the first time the sound of trucks in the wilderness, he had joined the fight for what he believed in. To the Park Service's good fortune, and mine, he joined our ranks as an NPS employee. He became my assistant, although he knew a thousand times more about northern Alaska than I could ever grasp. Philosophically we were in close agreement. We headed west together to see if the Kogoluktuk–Shungnak–Ambler river region, still designated for retention as federal land, should and could be added back into the park.

From the upper Shungnak, we made a circular hike over to the upper Kogoluktuk, down a ways into the Noatak's watershed, then over Blind Pass to a tributary of the Ambler. Was it all parkworthy? When we reached the Kogoluktuk Valley, Ray wrote:

The scenery was superb. The open forest offered sheltered camp-sites, while the mountains provided descending ridges for interested high country hikers. The crystal clear river was deep enough to supply hungry grayling for fishermen. Game trails indicated potential for wildlife photography. To the north the treeline ended quickly, and the river coursed through small canyons that encouraged exploration. Within eight miles of this spot one could select four side streams to ascend leading to passes into tributaries of the upper Noatak River. This is truly a unique recreational resource area.

On the north edge of the central Brooks Range, two big, handsome lakes, Kurupa and Cascade, provide an entrance into a splendid mountain region. Indeed, as glacial geologist Tom Hamilton had pointed out to us, it is unique to the central Brooks Range in that the entire sequence of glacial landforms, from ice, cirque, and stepped tarns down to morainal lakes, occurs within a two-day walk amid open terrain. With two lakes as departure points, it would be a splendidly important part of a national park. We checked it out, nevertheless, NPS botanist John Dennis and I, along with Dick Stenmark, and our expectations were indeed correct. Two Middlebury College students who helped us, Ned Farquhar and John Schubert, later distinguished themselves in a highly praised first biological survey of Alaska's Ray Mountains, and went on to win further environmental laurels.

Our evaluation was particularly important because the area was reserved both as potential parkland and for selection by the Native people. The Inupiat wanted it for its possible oil potential, so the lakes were omitted from the park. Later, when oil hopes faded, the Native corporation traded Kurupa (but not Cascade) to the park for more promising prospects elsewhere. Part of Native-selected Chandler Lake, also north of the Arctic Divide, was later traded into the park as well.

Getting to know the territory was more than a matter of geography; it was a matter of seasons as well. Veteran arctic dog musher that he is, Ray has said many times that, in the Brooks Range, summer is a lie. Winter is the truth. More and more people besides local residents are seeking on dogsled journeys and cross-country ski treks in early spring when light has returned but snow is still firm. Ray helped me to taste such an adventure mushing up the John River to Anaktuvuk Pass and beyond. Though but a brief experience, it was a sampler. On snowshoes, we often had to break trail for the dogs, and the sleds time and again rolled over in deep snow. They bucked and plunged across ice ridges, skidded on river flats. We bent into bitter winds, and found our feet soaked with frightening, freezing overflow. However, we also learned what a warm camp means after dogs are unharnessed and fed, and we sampled the exhilaration, the serene freedom, of gliding swiftly across a pure white world, sled runners purring behind flying paws and waving tails.

Then as at other times, as often as possible, we enjoyed meeting the people of the Brooks Range, learning of their needs and desires, appreciating their hospitality, trying to learn how we might best fit our protection goals to their culture.

I have mentioned that my Park Service colleagues and I dubbed Gates of the Arctic a black-belt park. It was to offer an experience to be worked up to, after seasoning from other outdoor endeavors of lesser stature. We saw the Alaskan parks, indeed all parks, as a spectrum of opportunities, just as a city park system needs football fields as well as rose gardens. Like certain especially challenging ski slopes, areas such as the Gates would be reserved "for experts only." Ruggedy mountains for ruggedy people, Bob Marshall's pal Ernie Johnson would have put it. And for responsible people who don't think they can just bop in and trash an area. If society were to develop a licensing system for outdoor use like that for automobile driving, Gates of the Arctic rangers could look closely for permit limitations and "points" against permit holders' records.

As Merrill Mattes noted in his 1968 reconnaissance, the Brooks Range actually is not all that formidable for travel afoot or afloat. Except for the high crags, one's progress is limited mainly by one's energy and endurance. There are no vast walls of crevassed ice fields, no uncrossable glacial torrents, few deserts of precarious boulders. It does not have the stupendous bigness of the Wrangells or Mount McKinley. Except for the places requiring mountaineering skills, the average hiker in fairly good condition can go much as he or she pleases. And it is not just for the young and hardy, as I think I demonstrated. Anyone reasonably active can enjoy it, and at one's own speed. Neither is it only for the leisured and well-to-do, another charge that was made by the enemies of park and wilderness status. Yes, one has to lay out a lot of cash for the airplane travel and invest in outdoor gear of good, lasting quality, but not nearly as much as would be expended in owning and driving a recreational vehicle around a circuit of meals and entertainment. And once one is afoot, expenses can amount to just a few dollars a day for food. There are working people of modest means who have saved for a long time to make the Brooks Range the trip of a lifetime. And it all can be done within the span of an average vacation.

Of course, the country is not the green golf course it appears to be when viewed from the air in summer. As described earlier, the tussocks, which look like mere nailheads from the sky, are the bane of a tundra walker, who can soon become exhausted in trying to cross a vast reach of tussockland. Even ordinary tundra, with only a modicum of tussock growth, is soft and hummocky, to be crossed with a spring-kneed half-stumbling gait that precludes rhythmic, confident striding. And

149

the walker must constantly beware of rocks and holes hidden beneath the vegetation. Only on well-packed gravel bars and on high, hard fell fields does the going become good.

Alder and willow thickets can further vex Brooks Range trekking. Although far fewer, smaller, and less luxuriant than those in more southerly parts of Alaska, these thickets cloak hillside drainages wherever there is ample moisture, particularly on south-facing slopes. Their branches usually lean downward, pressed in that direction by wind and snowpack, stretching horizontally for more light. When one is following the contour of a hillside, the thick branches present themselves like the bars of a cage, and climbing through them while carrying a pack, particularly an exterior-frame pack, is tedious and exasperating. Not only must every tough branch be fought with, but footing also is obscured. Often it is a deep-stream channel. A mile an hour through such a jungle is good going indeed. One companion of my Brooks Range travels strapped a souvenir caribou antler atop his pack, and his struggles through the thickets were appalling. We began making bets as to when he would give the antler up, but he persevered.

Encounters with alders and willows usually require decisions as to whether or not time and energy should be spent climbing steeply around them rather than fighting through. Hillside thickets often occur where a stream swings into a steep bluff, and following the water's edge is no longer possible. Then one must either ford or be forced up and over the bluff, often through the dense brush. If the stream is swollen, there is but one choice.

I hate and fear river crossings and, fortunately, have never been trapped by floodwaters as have been Marshall and many others who were forced to walk all the way around the tributary valley along steep hillsides or wait for days for the water to subside. If one cannot rock-hop across a stream, and if a quick splash-through is not worth the risk of soggy feet, then one must doff pack and change from boots to sneakers. This becomes tedious after a dozen stream crossings, and one is apt to say to hell with it, especially if boots are already half-wet from boggy tundra. As a wilderness traveler is absolutely dependent on the soundness of his feet, safeguarding boots is critical. Some of the newer boot materials help to solve this dilemma.

For larger rivers, Bob Waldrop taught my friends and me the technique of wading through in a group, holding hands for mutual support, bare-legged and in a line paralleling the current to minimize its drag. It is a bone-chilling business, especially when the river is still edged with ice and snow.

Despite the arduousness of wilderness travel, the major challenge of the Brooks Range is not its physical formidability but its remoteness, its vastness, and the stern vagaries of its weather. That is why it is not for the untrained and unwary, the ill-equipped, the out-of-shape, the casual, or the careless. Even map-reading requires careful thought, because the fifty-foot contours on most Brooks Range maps may hide a precipice in what can look like an easy pass.

Weather that can cause snow in summer or can suck out body heat with just-above-freezing dampness means that hypothermia stalks every journey. A broken leg a hundred trackless miles from help can mean agony and perhaps death, absent a rescuing angel airplane. So, every minute of every day, one must be extremely careful. In winter, the margin for error is zero. I have heard of only one recent fatality—a lone man who realized he couldn't make it out and took his own life. Perhaps the Brooks Range's reputation has discouraged the bop-in types. I hope it will continue to do so.

An added deterrent, of course, is the horde of mosquitoes. Someone has estimated that the total weight of arctic Alaska's mosquitoes exceeds that of its entire caribou population. I do not doubt it. Count the raindrops in a summer storm and they approximate the myriad mosquitoes. The early explorers have told of their great sufferings. A person crossing the tundra in summer without protection would die horribly. Fortunately, modern repellents, combined with adequate clothing and a tight, netted tent, can foil the bloodthirsty insects—though they are always present in a frenzied mass, dancing before one's face, waiting for the repellent to wear off. A slap on the knee can kill thirty or more. Sensing a warm body inside, they cling lustfully to tent netting, poking their probosci through the mesh. The few that do get inside whine in one's ears, waiting for their victims to sleep, to allow them at last a drink of blood.

But one can become acclimated to mosquitoes until, like the pattering raindrops, they seem just a normal part of the air, a part of life. They will crash into tea or soup, and that leads to jokes about lending the food a nuttier flavor and boosting its protein content.

I was extraordinarily lucky during my own Brooks Range journeys. The bugs did not drive me crazy. I was never rained on inordinately, nor nipped too severely by cold. Although I seemed forever to be tottering across unstable talus, heavy-laden with an unbalancing pack, I escaped injury save for one minor ankle twist. Never did I have to detour far, nor was I swept away by icy waters. I had a close call with a moose once, canoeing around a river bend in shallow water to find myself helpless before a moose calf and its protective mother—probably as dangerous a situation as one can get into with Alaskan wildlife. I held my breath and glided by, fearfully noting mama's laid-back ears and raised hair.

And I was never charged by a bear. No piece of writing on Alaska's wilds is complete, however, without its generally inconclusive dissertation on this subject of universal interest and concern. In Alaska, thoughts of bears can preoccupy the wilderness traveler the way sharks lurk in the mind of the ocean swimmer or fear of venomous fangs or squeezing coils can torment the explorer of swamp or jungle. Worry about bears sometimes becomes an obsession. Writer John McPhee confesses that in the Alaskan bush he "rarely thinks of anything else," and I am sure he is typical of many. Even my young wildernaut friend Macgill Adams, a guide deeply appreciative of all wildlife, once wrote in his journal after coming upon two young bears playing: "They were much more entertaining than the moose, *but* my philosophy is 'I'd rather not see'em.' It is uncomfortable to want to be an integral part of this place but share such an incongruous vibe about the bears. I don't like it, but I don't know how to think differently."

Statistics make clear the fact that one's chances of being hurt by a bear are far, far fewer than being struck by an auto almost anywhere, or being mugged on a city street, for that matter. We pursue our automotive, urban lives undaunted, often indifferent amid the police and ambulance sirens, but in the Alaskan wilderness we lie awake worrying about bears.

I speak particularly of the Alaskan brown, or grizzly bear, next to the polar bear the world's largest land carnivore. Brooks Range grizzlies do not grow to the huge size of the salmon-nourished brownies of the Alaska Peninsula and Southeast but they are big enough. Awesome, they loom like something out of the Ice Age, roaming their open range with imperial nonchalance.

Although no expert on the subject, I regard the smaller, ubiquitous black bear as more of a problem than the grizzly. The blacks, which inhabit the wooded regions of Alaska, are pests and marauders. They tend to hang around, or keep coming back for another foray. When provoked, they can be as dangerous to an unarmed person as a grizzly. Grizz generally wants no part of human association, but some of his kind were spoiled into dangerous moochers by oil pipeline workers. I hear that grizzlies are becoming a serious problem at last in the Brooks Range wilderness as more people come into it and are careless with their food.

Having never faced a grizzly's ire, I cannot titillate the reader with the harrowing bear stories so relished in books of Alaskan adventure. What few encounters I had were mild ones. The most dangerous has been described by Joe McGinniss in *Going to Extremes*. We had camped in a narrow canyon and were about to leave, scattered, packing up. I was off in the willows, literally caught with my pants down, when a sow grizzly and two cubs came roaming down the creekside. A pistol

152

The author plods up Blind Pass, out of the Noatak watershed toward that of the Ambler River. (National Park Service photograph by G. Ray Bane)

was our only firearm, and that was in a pack. Had the mother charged, we would not have been in a position even to put up a scare-off show. Fortunately, she ordered her cubs to scram up the hill, and all disappeared over the canyon rim.

Later on that trip, a helicopter pilot spotted us, and he and his passenger, an archaeologist whom we had hoped to see, landed. "Did you know that a bear was following you?" he asked. "We shooed him off." Perhaps that second bear was just curious. Grizzlies are, I have read. But we remembered opening tinned sardines for lunch. Wind must have wafted the aroma to Bruin's nostrils. Perhaps it was a bear spoiled by oil-camp kitchens. We were grateful not to find out.

Other occasions, most of them in camp, amounted only to knowledge of an ursine presence—stalking the other side of a creek, across a lake, on a far hillside, but always able to sidle in to join us. If walking, one can go the other way; with camp set, one can only keep tabs, quietly. In my case, all the bears evaporated. Once, at a lake in the De Long Mountains, three sows with cubs kept us pinned in camp all day. We were sure that they knew of us and would probably come rummaging into camp

153

if we departed on our scheduled explorations. They kept their distance, however, taught their cubs to fish, administered a little parental disciplining, and, by morning, had departed.

On the subject of bears, I have found that one of the most perplexing dilemmas is whether or not one should go armed in the Alaskan wilderness. Most bush Alaskans are never without a firearm, although there are notable exceptions among people who have had much experience with wild animals. "I'm glad to see you have a gun," a bush pilot remarked as he loaded us up for a flight into the upper Noatak. "Many hiking parties don't, but you'll notice that those of us who live out here always do."

There are valid arguments against being armed, both philosophical and practical. Lugging a gun, day after day, is a tedious nuisance, and there seems to be general consensus that handguns, even .357 and .44 magnums, are virtually useless when having to kill a grizzly bear. Rifles need to be exceptionally powerful, although skilled Natives have successfully hunted bears with very light weapons. If one is not a practiced, cool-headed marksman, a rifle shot is risky. The general choice for handiness, reliability, and power, is a 12-gauge shotgun of the riot-gun variety, loaded with slugs and/or buckshot, though even a shotgun requires proficiency. The gun packs a tremendous wallop at close range, but its effective range is so limited that it precludes long-distance shots that might merely wound an animal and change a dangerous situation to a deadly one.

I must admit to a certain peace of mind when curled up for the night with a private cannon nearby, its chamber safely empty but its magazine full. Confidence in one's defensive ability may lead to a grave problem, however. According to Andy Russell, expert bear hunter and photographer and author of *Grizzly Country*, a bear will know if a person is armed. Being so gives the human a certain subconscious truculence detectable by the animal, which in turn may match it. With the subtle arrogance of a firearm, the human being courts aggression. "Walk softly but carry a big stick," did Theodore Roosevelt once advise? Well, if one carries a big stick, perhaps one cannot walk softly enough, at least for bears.

If a bear is charging at me, and I have a gun, do I shoot? When? Those are agonizing, split-second, life-and-death decisions to contemplate. Many bear charges are bluffs. A Park Service photographer friend told me he has been charged to within ten feet, before the bear turned suddenly away. Had he been armed and had panicked and shot at twenty feet, a raging though dying bear might well have crashed into him. Maybe it is better not to have a choice, not to be able to shoot and perhaps bring on a disaster that might have passed. I don't know. I have been told that all confronted animals, no matter how dangerous, would prefer to go the other way than to attack.

There would seem to be obvious exceptions: animals sick or starving, surprised, perceiving their young or their food to be threatened. Or crossing that critical boundary of their personal space that triggers their only other defense: attack. I would rather go the other way first, very quietly.

But if attack does indeed come and there is no defense, a human must stand fast. It is the only hope if no tree is handy, and in the Brooks Range trees are few and spindly. Never, never, never run. To run away is to be prey. I've never heard an argument against that advice, which comes from every experienced hunter or naturalist I have met or read.

Considering all the risks and the generalities of animal behavior, maybe the best way out of the bear dilemma is, *carefully*, to take one's chances, just as one does every time one steps into that tin tent with the wheels on it. Bears are an essential part of Alaska's wilderness, and risk is implicit in wilderness living. Without risk, it is make-believe. If the bear keeps coming, well, remember a remark of Averill Thayer, often faced and followed by bears but never armed in all his years afield as manager of the Arctic National Wildlife Range: "If you've got to die—and you do—what a way to go! It's got class!"

From any span of time spent in wonderful country, however short or long or piecemeal, special memories linger in the mind to be savored over and over again. I say savored, for unless one has had particularly harrowing, mind-scarring times, the good ones win out over the bad, sweet over sour in the distillations of memory. Sometimes they stand out boldly or in radiance, still vibrant with excitement: a splendor of mountains, a torrent of birds, a caribou tide. Or they may be but an ambience recalled, a spirit, an aura, a mood created out of light and shadow, form and pattern, timbre and rhythm. Whether they be an event or just a condition, at one time or at many, they have imbued life with serenity, peace, exhilaration, reverence, or ecstasy abrim with tears.

Such magic charges the long-lit air of America's ultimate mountains. Close eyes and see remembered rainbows. Gargoyle crags lean high, and great voids of space yawn and beckon. But do not overlook the detail of plant and shrub arranged to make even a Japanese gardener gasp. Remember that shady channel with grayling leaping, the solitary tarn, that highest cirque with the eerie ice above, the falls below, roaring? Yes, all those, and a cathedral solitude, vaulted with a misty sky.

As the 1970s wore on, the time for planning waned. The Alaskan conservation proposals crystallized into legislation, and recommendations became refinements or last-chance tries to convince the executive and legislative powers that there would be a better conservation package if certain modifications were made. Planning turned to supporting bills in Congress, with Alaska fighting them all the way. When the huge land withdrawals faced expiration and still the Congress was debating the issues, Secretary of the Interior Cecil Andrus and President Jimmy Carter had to resort to executive powers to keep the disputed land closed to mining, and much of it was proclaimed as national monuments—seventeen in all. A national coalition of environmental groups, working with their proconservation congressional leaders, kept hoping and working for a better piece of Alaska lands legislation such as was offered in the House of Representatives.

However, those hopes were dashed along with those of President Carter for his reelection. A take-it-or-leave-it proposal in the Senate was accepted as the best that was going to happen. And, while not ideal, it was impressive. Most of the Brooks Range was placed in protective enclaves. In the east, the Arctic National Wildlife Range was doubled in size, its last word changed to *Refuge*. Far to the west, the extremities of the range became two of the many units of the Alaska Maritime National Wildlife Refuge: Cape Lisburne and Cape Thompson. The former was specially named to honor Ann Stevens, wife of Alaska's senior senator, and victim of an airplane crash. She had been very fond of the Cape Lisburne area and had worked with the Inupiat there. Cape Thompson, ironically, had been the scene of the Atomic Energy Commission's attempt in the 1960s to blast a deep-water port at the village of Chariot with a nuclear device. Outraged Inupiat helped to stop it.

Farther south on the coast, a Cape Krusenstern National Monument was established as a unit of the National Park System because of the exceptionally rich archaeological values there. In the western and central Brooks Range, a Kobuk Valley National Park was established, with a small portion of it designated as Wilderness. All of the Noatak Basin not selected by the Inupiat people was placed in a Noatak National Preserve, and declared to be entirely Wilderness. Adjoining it on the east and extending to the Trans-Alaska Oil Pipeline corridor, a Gates of the Arctic National Park and Preserve was also established, with most of it immediately placed in the National Wilderness Preservation System. The old Arctic National Wildlife Range territory was designated wilderness as well, except for most of its coastal plain, critical to wildlife but to be studied for oil potential. However, by citing the lack of a formal study, Alaska's politicians were able to deny wilderness protection to the huge refuge addition designed to give wilderness animals like the caribou a reliable habitat and migration routes.

Segments of ten arctic rivers were named to the National Wild and Scenic Rivers System: not only the Sheenjek, Wind, and Ivishak in the Arctic National Wildlife Refuge, but also the North Fork of the Koyukuk, the Tinayguk, John,

Alatna, Kobuk, Noatak, and Salmon, farther west. In addition, a lower reach of the Sheenjek, the Nigu-Etivluk, the Colville, the Utukok, and the Squirrel were designated for wild river study. A great tragedy of the whole wild river protection effort in Alaska was a political decision to look only at rivers within federally owned territory. If the lands were selected or slated for selection by the state of Alaska or by Native corporations, the rivers therein were not considered. As a result, the protected status of a splendid wild river ends abruptly at a place along its course not at all influenced by the river's character or quality. This policy ignored the definitive National Wild and Scenic Rivers Act of 1968, which looked at the stature and quality of the rivers, not at who happened to own the surrounding countryside. In fact, one long section of the act is devoted to how private property along a Wild, Scenic, or Recreational River is to be treated in the context of riverscape protection.

Some of the fine print in the Alaska National Interest Lands Conservation Act (ANILCA) of 1980 caused concern among the national coalition of conservation organizations whose efforts had put the bill on President Carter's desk, but the general rejoicing over what the big print did to protect nearly a third of Alaska for posterity drowned out the state of Alaska's whining. As the president signed the bill into law, he said:

> *Never before have we seized the opportunity to preserve so much of America's natural and cultural heritage on so grand a scale. . . . I've seen firsthand some of the splendors of Alaska. But many Americans have not. Now, whenever they or their children or their grandchildren choose to visit Alaska, they'll have the opportunity to see much of its splendid beauty undiminished and its majesty untarnished.*
>
> *Let us celebrate. The mountains . . . the rivers and lakes that harbor salmon and trout, the game trails of caribou and grizzly in the Brooks Range, the marshes where our waterfowl summer—all these are now preserved, now and, I pray, for all time to come.*

Cape Lisburne, end of the Brooks Range. (U.S. Fish and Wildlife Service photograph by Art Sowls)

EPILOGUE

What disappears with a debasement of wild landscapes is more than genetic diversity . . . or a chance for personal revitalization on a wilderness trip. We stand to lose the focus of our ideals. We stand to lose our sense of dignity, of compassion, even our sense of what we call God.

—Barry Lopez

While I look with pride on the growth of the land, it stirs me too with a feeling of sadness, for since the day when the foot of the first discoverer felt American soil, the wilderness has always been there to challenge American courage and to stimulate our nation's imagination; but when Alaska is civilized we will have turned the last page in the winning of our great country, and the first chapter in the book of our national destiny will be finished.

For this reason I could wish that America might always have an untamed Alaska.

Belmore Browne, president of the Camp Fire Club of America, wrote those words three-quarters of a century ago. In 1980, when the Alaska National Interest Lands Conservation Act was signed, it appeared as if his wish had at last come true. The law so intended it, it seemed. Now, however, little more than a decade after President Carter prayed that much of Browne's "untamed Alaska" was preserved "for all time to come," the ultimate wilderness of the Brooks Range that *had* to last because it *was* the last, is already showing sorry signs of wear. Threats to the Arctic's integrity loom on every side, and the time bombs of private inholdings are starting to detonate.

A seminal reason for this overarching problem is that when Congress voted to preserve "unrivaled scenic and geologic values . . . wildlife species . . . wilderness resource values . . . and maintain opportunities for scientific research in undisturbed ecosystems," Congress lied. Not in the personal, intentional sense, of course, but politically. It gainsaid through political compromise, much that the law had promised and which had been hoped for by millions of Americans. Masked by the noble rhetoric of preservation was the fact that ANILCA, great achievement though it was, had been flyblown by the Alaskan forces that had fought it so bitterly for nine years. They were able to tell their constituents that they had extracted from ANILCA almost all the advantages they had sought.

Celebrated as a great conservation coup, ANILCA is also now regarded by many as a monstrosity, 180 pages long, that confused its would-be implementers with all sorts of strange new provisions. As an old-time radio comedian once said of legal documents, "The big print gives it to you; the little print takes it away." In ANILCA, the little print countermanded the intent of preservation, protected the status quo of a variety of state and private property rights and mechanical access rights, and undermined conservation precedent. Native corporations had already run off with selection rights to areas which had critical protection needs, as had the state of Alaska.

As manager of the huge Arctic National Wildlife Refuge under this majestic but emasculated legislation, the U.S. Fish and Wildlife Service faced a dilemma: The coastal calving grounds of its principal wards, the Porcupine caribou herd, had been excised from wilderness status pending further studies and legislation that could open the area to oil exploration and development. Moreover, one of the political stratagems that confounded protection by ANILCA was to deny wilderness status to all the lands added to the old Arctic National Wildlife Range—lands where undisturbed habitat was critical. The refuge managers also found themselves having to manage human as well as animal migrants, as people flocked in to see the animals and birds before possible oil development could threaten them.

The National Park Service, in its limited role on the fringe of the National Park System before ANILCA, had never stood particularly tall in Alaska. Certainly the service bore little resemblance to a Royal Canadian Mounted Police for parks. Neither had it manifested the intrepidity of the U.S. Geological Survey. Now it was called upon to manage a strange new breed of parks and preserves in ways it was not trained for. The service was used to the "real" parks of the Lower Forty-Eight, where the rules were clear and long established, and "hard" parks where hunting, even for subsistence, was out of the question, and where Native people were usually artifacts of the past rather than a living part of the ecosystem. Most significant, it was largely a people-managing agency. Along with resource protection, its job was to ensure public enjoyment, with numbers of visitors more influential in determining budgets and professional advancement than acres or animals safekept. By tradition it has not been the ideal guardian of solitude.

Unable or unwilling to hire and train local people, even though ANILCA so directed, the NPS relied on imports from other kinds of parks, and its management tended to be both conventional and timid. There were some notable early mistakes. With American flag flying and an aluminum motorboat at the ready to catch poachers, uniformed rangers attempted to make visitor contacts along the Noatak. Surprised canoers there had savored the thought that they were traveling a remote wild waterway in a great biosphere reserve.

Upon encountering a guides' semipermanent camp (eventually dismantled) in the Gates of the Arctic, some wilderness walkers reported that their feeling of being in wild country was "dissolved completely. The wilderness we had looked forward to for years, the wilderness we had come more than 2,300 miles to find, the wilderness we thought we would find in the Brooks Range and nowhere else on this continent, simply did not exist."

It is small wonder, however, that federal land managers have been baffled and cowed, given the political leadership, federal and state, frowning down on them. Ever on the side of machines, roads, real estate development, and rife tourism, this vengeful political establishment has been determined to unravel Alaskan conservation as much as possible, and it has watched the accommodations in ANILCA undercut the act's basic purpose. When the presidency changed hands soon after the law was enacted, clever foes of Alaskan conservation were appointed to places of power from which they could further obstruct or weaken wilderness protection and values and champion development. Now they were foxes set to guard the henroost of Alaskan wildlands. In one example of their iniquity, they forced the NPS to recommend against further wilderness protection for Gates of the Arctic National Park and Preserve after permitting it to acclaim wilderness as "*the* special value" of the region.

Individual public land managers in Alaska, and elsewhere, have been both politicized and intimidated, bullied and cashiered, if they have stood their professional ground. Naturally, therefore, the career advancement process has tended to select for circumspection and acquiescence. When courage and tough-mindedness are liabilities, few dare stand in righteous guardianship.

So, how fares the Brooks Range today? Although arctic Alaska is still big, still beautiful, still challenging, the freshness has faded. Tents dot the landscape in favorite valleys. Vehicle and even foot trails scar the land. So does the residue of hunters' camps. Snow machines and motorboats joyride across wilderness lands and waters. Airplanes flit in and out like dragonflies, making the Brooks Range one of the most accessible wildernesses in the world.

Now come all-terrain vehicles (ATVs) that are threatening fragile environments all over Alaska—"like an invasion of fire ants," as one Alaskan put it. They are used in the Arctic National Wildlife Refuge for legal access to private inholdings. From Anaktuvuk Pass in the central Brooks, an oil-supported city—but one where the more than 250 residents still subsist on caribou and sheep—tracks from six- and eight-wheel ATVs radiate like strands of a spiderweb, scarring the tundra for miles. The wild upper Anaktuvuk River Valley I walked two decades ago is now a roadway, I am told. The federal government does not regard ATVs as traditional subsistence equipment, and they are banned from parkland. The Native people have asserted that ATVs *do* qualify as legitimate subsistence devices, however, and they have often used them to stray from reserved rights-of-way across the park. After much argument, the NPS and the Nunamiut are considering a complex land exchange, itself controversial, that would allow overall ATV use but only in a specified part of the park, so as to contain such use permanently within the agreed-upon area. In a dynamic living system like subsistence hunting and gathering, one must wonder if such use can be so permanently limited.

As for recreational use—hiking and boating—the spectacular Arrigetch Peaks area in Gates of the Arctic National Park was heavily impacted early on. So has been the popular Noatak River, by campsite scars proliferating along the banks, the fish in headwaters lakes have been depleted. One canoeman had twelve other parties pull in behind his at a favorite Noatak camping place. Bears have been attracted to the food taken into the wilderness by increasing numbers of visitors, who must now carry heavy bear-proof containers. Concern for safety has even caused some land closures where bear problems have been deemed severe.

Use in the Arctic National Wildlife Refuge, particularly river float trips, has increased sevenfold, and trip scheduling on favorite rivers seems now to be necessary. The U.S. Fish and Wildlife Service has reported that

> *along the more popular rivers, crowding, site damage, and litter are beginning to erode the qualities for which the refuge is renowned. Increasingly, visitors complain that their expectations for wilderness, naturalness, solitude and adventure are not being met. Some users are asking the agency to protect ecological and experience values related to the rivers and to do so in a manner that is as equitable and unobtrusive as possible.*

Guides are complaining also, and speak of jockeying for campsites.

As early as 1984, a survey of visitors to Gates of the Arctic National Park found most of them concerned about threats to the region's wild character, having encountered trash, fire rings, camps and cabins, and other signs of human activities. A park official recently estimated that more than $1 million would be required to clean up the trash, old and new, accumulated in the central Brooks Range.

The General Management Plan for Gates of the Arctic honored nearly all of the precepts planned for this ultimate wilderness park, at least in the ideal. Limitations have been set on the size of parties traveling in the park areas, and in the refuge as well, because of the impact a single large group has. But the cornerstone of all the park planning was abandoned. That was the proposed system of reservations and permits designed to *prevent* wear and tear of the park by limiting use, if need be, and deploying visitors so that each individual, each group, could find unsoiled solitude.

The abandonment was not surprising. After all, Alaska's senior senator had complained to President Carter at the ANILCA signing that "we seek to protect our freedoms, to try to prevent us from becoming a 'permit society.' " Moreover, the Park Service, with its mandate to provide public enjoyment, does not like to say no to visitors. Consequently, for a park where less than two thousand visitors a year are already causing perceptible damage, the NPS has predicted eighteen thousand by the year 2010! Although the law requires the determination of carrying capacities for parks, that has not been done. The land managers seem to have neither the capability nor the will to determine or enforce such limits. If capacities are set and limits adhered to, the politics of trying to roll back use will be horrendous, for use is encouraged by commercial enterprises that stand to lose income if their operations are curtailed. Politics, which watches over business far more vigilantly than over wilderness, cannot, alas, look a century ahead at the delegation it could prevent.

With no policies or mechanisms for control short of a disaster, the NPS apparently has had to adopt the management principle known as acceptable rate of change, with use and development patterns left to evolve without strict adherence to standards. Under that approach, gradual degradation of landscape and dilution of experience would not be noted as being reprehensible, or even as a serious deprivation. We human beings are adaptable creatures, making the best of what we find and little wondering what excellence might have been lost. Perhaps we can take meager comfort from the fact that the early damage is the most noticeable. Additional damage becomes less and less conspicuous until it is accepted as normal, a matter of course.

In the absence of any firm control by Brooks Range land managers over use of the land under their stewardship, the commercial guides and outfitters have largely taken over. Through their business promotion, they influence who enters the country, when and where, although they are discouraged from promoting repetitive, "canned" trips. With no advance notification of trips required, let alone permission, the NPS and the Fish and Wildlife Service rarely know who is in their territory until after the fact.

With the reassurance and convenience of outfitters' services, more and more Brooks Range visitors are being led rather than self-motivated to venture on a private quest. Those still seeking a private exploration and experience are beginning to fear that scheduling of the commercial outfitters will leave no room for them.

In fairness, many of the guides, particularly the locally based ones, warrant appreciation and approval of the high standards by which they operate. Many care but for a modest living from a life they love. They cherish the wilderness, and they teach their clients good conduct there. They also serve as eyes and ears for the small park and refuge staffs. Some speak up in favor of limiting licenses as well as number and size of trips.

Anyone can become an outfitter who registers, has insurance, and pays a modest fee, however, and those in the business have proliferated, some coming from as far away as the East Coast. Limiting them in the parklands would require a concessions system, with outfitters bidding for the privilege and guaranteed the opportunity for a reasonable profit. If larger operators come onto the fragile arctic scene, if guaranteed concessions are allotted, the small, personal guiding operations may be brushed aside. The politics of profit, under the banner of tourism, could well cause solitude to become a vanished value in the Brooks Range.

The Northern Alaska Environmental Center in Fairbanks has expressed grave concern over substantial private inholdings in the Arctic National Wildlife Refuge. "The potential subdivision, sale, and commercial development of the inholdings may be the greatest long-term threat to the wilderness character of the rivers," the center has declared.

Such private inholdings command strategic parts of the central Brooks Range as well. The thousands of acres of small tracts on lakes and at river confluences are real estate time bombs that eventually may destroy the wilderness qualities of huge areas, turning country reserved for natural functioning and for exploration into a settled land. It was crucial that they be eliminated—bought at the outset of public management, with generous prices paid to prevent charges of landowner persecution. Given the long-term costs to the public of letting these holdings remain—costs of lost wilderness and the huge price of eventual buyout when they become intolerable—almost any price paid would be a bargain in the long run.

Short-term private interests prevailed over the ongoing public purpose of protecting an arctic wilderness, however. All private developments in Gates of the Arctic National Park except the most egregious of mining operations were declared "compatible" with the wilderness park, even when they stuck out like pimples on the landscape and were magnets for human impact upon the land. Interest in building cabins is increasing, and that may portend ATV access to more wild country. An existing cabin on one exquisite lake reportedly is being leased and expanded into a commercial enterprise.

On the north and south, the Brooks Range is flanked by fourteen big lakes, beautiful in themselves and beautiful points of departure. Most were selected either by the state of Alaska or by Native corporations. Wild Lake, perhaps the most beautiful, already boasts a subdivision; Iniakuk, a commercial lodge, with a companion facility deep in the parkland. The state decided to sell off lots from its land on Chandalar Lake, close under the Arctic National Wildlife Refuge. Some five thousand acres of such Brooks Range holdings were scheduled for sale over a two-decade period. This was reported in the Anchorage *Daily News* magazine in a special two-article series entitled "The Selling of the Brooks Range," with the subheading, "The Brooks Range up for grabs." The second article focused on conservationists' "selling" the range for a park, resulting in overuse because there was publicity but no controls.

"Some places are, and always must be, special—unchanged monuments to the natural beauty and economy of wild places and wild things. They must be protected, for they cannot be restored. They must be left alone, for they cannot be improved." So rang an editorial in the *Daily News*, angry at the idea of selling off land that should belong in common to all generations of Alaskans.

"Subdividing the Brooks Range, even a small corner of it, is like franchising vendors in the temple, or paving over a burial ground . . . robbing Fort Knox or trashing the Bill of Rights," the editorial thundered. "It cannot be tolerated today because it cannot be taken back tomorrow. This generation must safeguard the Brooks Range for all those that follow."

Apparently, many of the private inholdings can now be purchased, but there is no federal money for that. Even with funds available, the governmental buying process, requiring as much as a year just to obtain an appraisal, is so ponderous that once-willing sellers have changed their minds. They are especially prone to do so when they receive appraisals that they consider too conservative. Not only does the government need more liberal buy-out policies, but the Brooks Range also desperately needs the help of privately managed trust funds with which to buy promptly and generously when property is offered. Such a land trust could operate as a revolving fund, buying property whenever available, holding it for the government to purchase, and then repeating the process.

The state is asserting ownership of all navigable waters in the federal reserves, plus the access rights thereto. This could make a joke of the National Wild and Scenic River designations, allowing uses on rivers as well as lakes, that would be completely incompatible with wilderness. River bottoms might even be mined.

Now come roads. Under an 1866 law, Revised Statute 2477, now repealed but with preexisting rights still valid, Alaska is identifying some 1,400 traditional rights-of-way throughout the state that it asserts it can claim and develop into roads. One is the Hickel Highway, the now-sodden winter road once bulldozed up the John River to Anaktuvuk Pass. A western route across the southern flanks of the Brooks Range to the Kobuk River, Ambler, and beyond was provided for in ANILCA. The beginning of that, a road from the Dalton Highway to Evansville and Bettles Field, reportedly is already budgeted as a top priority of the state, aided by federal highway money. If roads insinuate themselves into this last big wilderness, can hotels, tourism, and all its pressures be far behind? Elaborate recreation management plans for the Dalton Highway as promulgated by the Bureau of Land Management forecast nearly fifty thousand visitors annually in the next ten years if the road is opened all the way to the Arctic Coast. Already, the public can drive as far as the Brooks Range. Retaining the range's wilderness integrity, keeping its Wild Rivers wild, may well require strong and determined legal defenses.

The emasculation of ANILCA, Alaska's development schemes, and the press of an insatiable population may have set the stage for forms of arctic development that could soon wipe out our ultimate wilderness resource. A young friend who has spent much time in arctic Alaska wrote me recently:

> *I hope that your book, and the writings of other environmentalists, can help, and will not merely serve as epitaphs for our wild country. Unfortunately, I am now getting increasingly more pessimistic about the future of the Arctic. I know of no environmentalist who feels good about the state of affairs. We have an increasing number of developers, recreationists, researchers, park and refuge employees, hunters, Natives, etc. who are demanding access to our public land and resources. . . . I'm afraid that we have a basic problem that precludes a happy ending. I'm starting to understand that our economy is completely based on and reliant upon growth [and] . . . will ace out our wild areas,*

one after another. They will shrink, becoming smaller and increasingly more compromised and all the while surrounded by more, closer developed areas. Then our ever-growing population will finish them off by using them as escapes, as playgrounds, until they no longer resemble wild areas. I see it gradually (or rapidly) happening to every wild place. . . . It's all pretty sad.

Marvin Mangus, veteran arctic geologist, corroborated this in a letter of his own. "The last of the Frontier is gone," he said; "too many Boy Scouts and Carpet Baggers." But then he noted a far broader and more insidious threat to a pristine Arctic: "The smog from Europe and Asia is really noticeable." Added to that smog are millions of tons of pollutants spewed by Alaskan oil developments into the once clear arctic air.

In his collection of essays, *The Practice of the Wild*, Gary Snyder has indicated that lamenting a lost frontier may be misdirected, that something far more awesome, epochal is closing for mankind. "The condition of life in the Far North approaches the experience of the hunter-gatherer world, the kind of world that was not just the cradle but the young adulthood of humanity," he has noted.

The north still has a wild community, in most of its numbers, intact. There is a relatively small group of hardy individuals who live as hunters and foragers and who have learned to move with mindful intensity that is basic to elder human experience. It is not the 'frontier' but the last of the Pleistocene in all its glory of salmon, bear, caribou, deer, ducks and geese, whales and walruses, and moose. It will not, of course, last much longer.

But amid such despairful adieux, one group of Native Americans keeps up its courage and its hope. They are the Gwich'in Athapaskans, America's northern-most Indian nation, only a few thousand in number and scattered across arctic Alaska and Canada from the Chandalar to the Mackenzie River. They have been fighting heroically against oil development in the Arctic National Wildlife Refuge. From mythic time, they have been people of the caribou. They say that every one of them has a bit of caribou heart, just as every caribou heart is partly human. "Why risk the future of the caribou?" they ask. "The birthplace of these animals, this we cannot touch."

"This is not just an environmental issue," one village elder has explained. "It is about the survival of an ancient culture that depends on caribou. It's not just what we eat; it is who we are. Caribou are our life. It is in our stories and songs and the whole way we see the world." Another has added, "We are part of the ongoing process of the planet. When we run out of planet, then what?"

The Gwich'in have confirmed their determination to defend the calving grounds that big oil is ogling. At Arctic Village in 1988, meeting as an entire nation for the first time in a century, they founded a Gwich'in Steering Committee to protest in Washington, D.C., and Ottawa against meddling with the birth zone of a species that has roamed the Arctic for more than fifty thousand years. A united Gwich'in have stood up to the secretary of the interior and sued him, for as one leader put it, "Our route to God is through the caribou."

For their pains, Alaska's Gwich'in were left off the eight-member International Porcupine Caribou Board, though they account for more than 80 percent of the Porcupine caribou harvest. In their stead, two Inupiat were appointed. They represent a people pragmatically in favor of oil development and equivocal toward their ancestral land ethic, though of course they ask that the development proceed carefully. The Inupiat are concerned more with the fate of sea mammals, which they equate with the Athapaskans' caribou.

Despite being left off the board, the Gwich'in Nation will continue to address international caribou matters anyway—and in Alaska. They have founded their own International Caribou Commission and have codified their hunting management traditions. They are discussing the possibility of an international bicultural reserve, a "Caribou Commons" of World Heritage rank. With sufficient international commitment, the Arctic and Yukon Flats national wildlife refuges, Yukon Park, and extensive protected areas in arctic Canada *together* could make the largest protected region of its kind in the world.

If a tiny but undaunted, undespairing Gwich'in Nation can courageously defend arctic Alaska at great cost and effort, even when many of its people are disoriented by such culture-cracking social and economic problems as alcoholism, drugs, and scarce paychecks, *so can ours.* ANILCA, flawed though it be, still contains plenty of protective authority, for it is rooted in older, stronger law, such as the organic act of the National Park Service. ANILCA makes clear that park, refuge, and wilderness values are to be perpetuated, and of course the act can be vastly strengthened by amendment. Some of its present provisions may weaken Brooks Range protection, but conditional, "unless" language also is amply present in that law to undergird its protective intent. Example: The weakening may take effect "unless [the secretary of the interior] finds in writing that such program or recommendations violates recognized principles of wildlife conservation . . . [or] is contrary to the purposes for which the park . . . is established." Also, the secretary must always consider "the specific purposes for which the concerned conservation system unit was established or expanded."

Of course, we must always make sure that we have a gallant secretary of the interior, appointed by an equally conservation-minded president to stand like Horatius at the bridge, shield braced and sword drawn in defense of America's natural heritage.

We Americans often regard landmark acts of Congress as great deeds completed, grand dedications following which we need worry no more. Our temperament does not enjoy constant oversight and tending. It is more exciting for us to design than to maintain. Yet tend we must to keep the accomplishments we have achieved. On the ground in Alaska (as elsewhere), we must make sure that the managers of our national lands do their duty, carrying out the plans and enforcing the rules and standards. Virtue does not always come with a green uniform. We should celebrate the NPS professionalism, however, and defend its ranks from political pressure. If we support the men and women set to guard our parks, our refuges, our wilderness, our Brooks Range, insisting that their superiors back them up, they will more likely muster the necessary gumption to watch over our wild treasures well.

We have not really lost the glory and challenge of the Brooks Range—not yet, anyway. There are still bear prints and wolf tracks on the strand, and the caribou stream by the thousands across the mountains. Only lacking is the courage and commitment to hand it all on, intact and untainted.

And why? Well, if we destroy all natural systems, there will be no baselines to show us how far we have strayed from the natural scheme of things, to let us sense our roots. Also, although we are social animals, places of quiet, places to be alone, with opportunities to look and listen, around and within, have always been needed and valued by humanity. We must keep within adequate American wilderness what Bob Marshall and other founders of The Wilderness Society called "the environment of solitude."

According to a psychologist, Robert A. Hanson, whom I once met in Alaska, wilderness, with its absence of man-made objects, seems to be the one place left where exploration still generally functions and is meaningful as outdoor challenge and a means to mental health. "Throughout many thousands of years of evolutionary history man built upon his psychological characteristic of exploration," Hanson has written.

Here an individual or group can rediscover the thrill, excitement, and fascination inherent in exploration, while leaving the land undisturbed for others to follow and repeat the experience.

The growth of our urban areas and increasing population levels require that we keep an adequate availability of wilderness areas to enable man to . . . deepen his ties to his environment.

And what about the rights of the land itself, the land and *all* its creatures? Mardy Murie has asked, "Having been the basis of all our sophisticated society, doesn't wilderness itself have a right to live on?"

Let us end in hope; begin to hope with Gary Snyder, who has written: "Something of Alaska may survive by converting its newly arrived Euro-American population into postindustrial wilderness lovers by the magic of its casual danger, all-day darkness, all-night light, emptiness, uselessness, facelessness, frozen breath, smoked fish."

Snyder also has noted that "we need a civilization that can live fully and creatively with wildness. We must start growing it right here, in the New World." Therefore, let us not write an epitaph but help to answer a president's prayer that the Brooks Range, along with much else in the Great Land of Alaska, *be* preserved for all time to come. Despite our diversity of values and our difficulty in integrating them, assistance can emanate from all the people in the world who are realizing what these ultimate mountains mean to the Earth and her many children, mountains that can continue to display the untorn fabric of creation. Perhaps all of the Arctic can be a great world biosphere reserve, a *respected* one. Perhaps we can even aspire to returning it to the state Bob Marshall described: "so peaceful and pure . . . a pattern for the Eden of men's dreams."

The Brooks Range

In seeding cotton, now, the sedges nod,
Gracefully impudent before the stark austerity.
How short ago unending, aerie song poured out a quietude.
Constellated flowers spangled the land
Under the long, the ever light, magically gilding.

Even now, a late blooming questions the calendar of cold.

As ptarmigan molt to winter white,
The high sheep's livery,
Another carpet soon will greet heraldic frost:
Scarlet and gold,
Spread north for antlered retinues.

Glazed rivers will be gainsaid:
Life flows despite congealing twilight,
Though shagginess will doze after the last berries shrivel,
And signaling fur nest down beneath the snows,
Where thin roots overlace the frozen muck, the stones.

Only the silent fur will bound across blue arctic dark,
Companion, competitor of silent feather,
Hunting toward bitter destinies
Until light-faithful buddings, breedings quicken again
Exquisitely, tenuously.

Does ice remember slicing mountains down,
Shaping cores for sun to knap with shadows?
Like wolves, the crags would howl.

Ice now can only pluck gaunt fossil seas.
Summer forces—mists, soft-wearing rains—
Seem kinder to the eon-dying.
Can they and unguent sun begin to heal
The torn wounds of spring?

Who heals the deeper wounds?
Who hears testimony against high spoiling intellects?
Who weighs respect?
Who notes reverence?
The Raven?
What reciprocity
Thanks life for life, with care?
The High Court is robed with cloud.
All rise!

One may also kneel.

J. M. K.

GEOGRAPHY

The interlocking ranges stretched across the Arctic in Yukon Territory and Alaska were once known as the Rocky Mountains. Sir John Franklin called them so as his ship sailed along the Arctic Coast in 1826, searching for the Northwest Passage.

It was an apt naming, if one considers that they are topographically an extension of the Rocky Mountain system that forms the Continental Divide. Near the Mackenzie River Delta, America's backbone bends west, however, and extends across arctic Canada and Alaska, subsiding after seven hundred miles into the waters of the Chukchi Sea.

It was not until 1925 that the range as a whole was named in honor of Alfred Hulse Brooks, chief Alaskan geologist of the United States Geological Survey for twenty-one years. It was he who first recognized that these mountains were different in origin from the Rockies. He proposed that they be termed the Arctic Mountain System.

To the Native people, the Inupiat Eskimos on the north and west, the Athapaskan Indians on the south, they were simply The Mountains, though each place of consequence had its own particular appellation. The Inupiat or Athapaskan names usually told of a characteristic of the place, what could be expected or found there, or what had happened there once upon a time.

Explorers and prospectors later gave names to major features, particular mountain chains—links or appendages of the more extensive mass—as well as to major rivers and lakes. A few of the names were descriptive, but most honored a person—a companion, perhaps, or a superior, or an admired notable far away.

Many of the peaks and ridges, streams and valleys, small lakes and tarns have not received names, except for a few unofficial ones, temporarily given for the convenience or frivolity of people using the area. Fortunately, these for the most part have not been recognized. Because nameless geography seems appealing and appropriate to this arctic fastness, it has become policy not to scatter nomenclature across the Brooks Range any more.

The principal names on the map refer to various discrete or semidiscrete ranges. After the Continental Divide turns west from the north–south-trending Richardson Mountains, the first low hills form the Barn Range. Then come the Buckland Hills, backed by the first snowy summits Sir John sighted. They became

173

patriotically known as the British Mountains, now crossed by the Alaska–Yukon Territory international boundary. The highest peak, at 7,240 feet, is Mount Greenough, named by Franklin for George Bellas Greenough, founder and first president of the London Geographical Society. Paralleling the British Mountains to the southwest are the Davidsons, named for a pioneer cartographer, later a professor of geodesy, George Davidson. His coastal survey work was far from the Arctic, but it influenced Congress to buy Alaska.

Beyond the Kongakut River Valley, the range swells upward as the Romanzof Mountains, apogee of the Brooks. Franklin wrote that his ship "had now arrived opposite the commencement of another range, which I named after the late Count Nicholas Romanzof, Chancellor of the Russian Emperor, as a tribute out of respect to the memory of that distinguished patron and promoter of discovery and science."

In the Romanzofs tower three of the range's highest peaks, Mounts Michelson, Hubley, and Isto. In the late 1950s, Isto was proclaimed the apex of arctic America, its height reported as 9,060 feet above sea level. Many charts mark it as 9,050. It had been called Mount Leffingwell after that intrepid early explorer of the region for whom a glacier on Mount Michelson is still named. Geologists have also given his name to a front ridge of the Romanzofs and a branch of the Aichillik River. A 1966 renaming of the peak honored engineer Reynold E. "Pete" Isto of the U.S. Geological Survey, who had died in a Colorado climbing accident. He pioneered the use of helicopters in Alaskan mapping. Renowned also as a mountaineer, Isto had made the first ascent of 8,855-foot Mount Michelson (named for the American scientist Albert Abraham Michelson) when it was thought to be the range's highest summit.

Across the valley of the Hulahula River (named by whalers with warm memories of Hawaiian sojourns) looms still another mountain mass. One of the British captains searching for the lost Franklin expedition, Thomas Simpson, wrote in 1843,

The portion at the Rocky Mountains visible from the coast does not terminate, as conjectured by Sir John Franklin, with the Romanzof chain. After a brief interval, another chain commences, less lofty, perhaps, but equally picturesque; which in honor of the distinguished officer whose discoveries we were following up, we named the Franklin Range.

The Franklin Range is dominated by Mount Chamberlin, which is named for Thomas Crowder Chamberlin, geologist with the Peary Auxiliary Expedition of 1894. In many ways it is the Brooks Range's most majestic mountain and now appears to be its sovereign peak. A more recent, more detailed map of the Mount Isto area has reduced that summit's stated height to 8,975 feet. That makes it only slightly higher than its neighbor, the 8,915-foot eminence named for glaciologist Richard Carleton Hubley. The 85-foot reduction in Mount Isto's height would seem to make Chamberlin, at 9,020 feet above sea level, the finial of the range. Further mapping revisions may again change the ranking, however, for the more detailed maps of the Chamberlin, Michelson, and Hubley areas are much older than that which reduced Isto's height. It is doubtful that the Brooks Range will care.

Guarding the Franklins on the north are two front ranges, the Shublik and Sadlerochit mountains—to the Inupiat, a "region outside the principal range."

Across the valley of the Canning River, the rugged gray ridges and summits of the Philip Smith Mountains extend to Atigun Pass, where the Trans-Alaska Oil Pipeline and parallel Dalton Highway slice through the Brooks Range. The name of the mountains honors Philip Sidney Smith, who succeeded Brooks as chief Alaska geologist from 1925–1946 and was an indefatigable explorer in the region.

Then comes the central Brooks Range, consisting mainly of the Endicott Mountains, named for William Crowninshield Endicott, President Cleveland's secretary of war. They include the 7,457-foot spire of Mount Doonerak, which explorer/forester Robert Marshall first dubbed the Matterhorn of the Koyukuk and thought to be the highest summit of the range. Marshall, who applied names to 164 sites of the region, later chose for the peak an Inupiat word for one of the innumerable, often devilish, spirits believed responsible for all that transpires on Earth.

The Endicotts become the Schwatkas around Mount Igikpak ("Big Mountain" or "Two Big Peaks"), the 8,510-foot citadel of granite that forms the hub of the central Brooks. Lieutenant Frederick Schwatka explored the Yukon River in 1883, and wrote extensively on Alaska. The range then splits on either side of the huge Noatak Basin. On the north, the De Long Mountains form the Arctic Divide that generally separates northward and westward drainages. Their name commemorates Lieutenant Commander George Washington De Long, U.S.N., commander of the ill-fated steamer *Jeannette,* which was crushed by ice in 1881. Small ranges nearer the Noatak include the Iggiruk, Kingasivik, Imikneyak, and Poktovik mountains.

The Noatak Basin is bounded on the south by the Baird Mountains, which separate it from the Kobuk Basin. They were named for a secretary of the Smithsonian Institution, Spencer Fullerton Baird, a naturalist noted for his bird studies.

These western Brooks Range mountains have flankers. On the north stretch the long whalebacks, Lookout Ridge and Archimedes Ridge. On the south stand the Alatna Hills, Helpmejack Hills, Akoliakruich Hills, Angayucham Mountains, Lockwood Hills, the Sheklukshuk Range, Waring Mountains, and Kiana Hills. Finally the Brooks Range sinks into the Chukchi Sea. The northwesternmost part of the Brooks Range are the Lisburne Hills, ending abruptly at Cape Lisburne. The Mulgraves stand west of the Noatak River, and, a little farther south, the lower Noatak slices through the Igichuk Hills, which back Cape Krusenstern.

BIBLIOGRAPHY

Many of the books cited here have their own bibliographies of valuable and interesting reading on the Brooks Range. The *Alaska Regional Profiles*, prepared by Lidia L. Selkregg and published by the University of Alaska's Arctic Environmental Information and Data Center, are an extraordinary bibliographical resource. They also contain a wealth of textual information, maps, graphs and pictures.

The Final Environmental Impact Statements on Brooks Range conservation proposals, published by the Department of the Interior in 1973, also have good bibliographies, as does G. Frank Williss' "Do Things Right the First Time": Administrative History of the National Park Service, and the Alaska National Interest Lands Conservation Act of 1980.

Melvin Ricks' Alaska Bibliography is annotated and encyclopedic, with 268 pages of citations. Many entries are cross-referenced and keyed to other bibliographical sources. Melvin B. Ricks (1896–1964) worked on the bibliography for more than a quarter of a century. After retirement from federal and state service, he became curator of the Cook Inlet Historical Society Museum shortly before his death. The bibliography was edited and updated in the early 1970s by Stephen W. and Betty J. Haycox for the Alaska Historical Commission, which published it in 1977. As the most comprehensive and complete bibliography dealing with Alaska subjects, literature, and authors, Professor Haycox and his wife cite the *Arctic Bibliography*, published since 1953 by the Arctic Institute of North America, Montreal, Canada, in cooperation with the U.S. Department of Defense.

Abbey, Edward. *Down the River.* E. P. Dutton. New York, NY, 1982.

Alaska Geographic Society—
"The Brooks Range." Vol. 4, No. 2 (1977).
"The Kotzebue Basin." Vol. 8, No. 3 (1981).
"Alaska National Interest Lands." Vol. 8, No. 4 (1981).
"Up the Koyukuk." Vol. 10, No. 4 (1983).

Alexander, Susan. "Arctic Walkabout." Wilderness, Vol. 50, No. 174 (1986).

Anderson, Douglas D.; Bane, G. Ray; Nelson, R. K.; Anderson, Wanni W.; and Sheldon, Nita. *Kuuvangmiut Subsistence: Eskimo Life in the Latter 20th Century.* U.S. Department of the Interior National Park Service. Brown University. Providence, RI, 1976.

Annabel, Russell. *Alaskan Tales.* A. S. Barnes and Company. New York, NY, 1953.

Beechey, Frederick William. *Narrative of a Voyage to the Pacific and Bering's Strait.* London, UK, 1831.

Berger, Thomas R.—
Village Journey: Report of the Alaska Native Review Commission. Farrar, Straus & Giroux. New York, NY, 1985.
Northern Frontier, Northern Homeland. Ministry of Supply and Services. Ottawa, Canada, 1977.
"The Berger Report: Northern Frontier, Northern Homeland—Highlights from a Landmark Canadian Document." *The Living Wilderness,* Vol. 41, No. 137 (April/June 1977).

Bliss, Lawrence C. and Gustafson, Karen M. "Proposed Ecological Natural Landmarks in the Brooks Range, Alaska." Department of Botany, University of Washington. Prepared for U.S. Department of the Interior Heritage Conservation and Recreation Service. Seattle, WA, 1981.

Brooks, Alfred H. and Others. *Mineral Resources of Alaska: Report on Progress of Investigations in 1911.* Department of the Interior. United States Geological Survey Bulletin 520. Washington, DC, 1912.

Brown, Chip. "An Encounter in the Brooks Range." The Living Wilderness, Vol. 41, No. 138 (July/ September 1977).

Brown, William E.—
This Last Treasure: Alaska National Parklands. Alaska Natural History Association. Anchorage, AK, 1982.
Gaunt Beauty . . . Tenuous Life. National Park Service. Historic Resources Study for Gates of the Arctic National Park, 1988.

Bruemmer, Fred. "Life Upon the Permafrost." Natural History Magazine (April 1987).

Cahn, Robert—
"Alaska: A Matter of 80,000,000 Acres." Audubon Magazine, Volume 76, Number 4 (July 1974).
"The Race to Save Wild Alaska." The Living Wilderness, Volume 41, Number 138 (July/August 1977).
The Fight to Save Wild Alaska. National Audubon Society. New York, NY, 1982.

Calef, George. *Caribou and the Barren-Lands.* Canadian Arctic Resources Committee. Ottawa, Ontario, Canada, 1981.

Cantwell, J. C., Third Lieutenant.—
"A Narrative Account of the Exploration of the Kowak River, Alaska, 1884." In *Report of the Cruise of the Revenue Marine Steamer* Corwin *in the Arctic Ocean in the Year 1884.* By Captain M. A. Healy, U.S.R.M., Commander. Government Printing Office. Washington, DC, 1889.
"A Narrative Account of the Exploration of the Kowak River, 1885." In *Report of the Cruise of the Revenue Marine Steamer* Corwin *in the Arctic Ocean in the Year 1885.* By Captain M. A. Healy, U.S.R.M., Commander. Government Printing Office. Washington, DC, 1887.

Cantwell, Robert. "The Ultimate Confrontation." Sports Illustrated (March 24, 1969).

Carnes, William G., ed. A Preliminary Geographical Survey of the Kongakut-Firth River Area, Alaska-Canada. United States Department of the Interior, National Park Service. Washington, DC, 1954.

Caulfield, Richard A. Subsistence Land Use in Upper Yukon-Porcupine Communities. Technical Paper Number 16 (June 1983). Alaska Department of Fish and Game Division of Subsistence.

Coles, Robert. *The Last and First Eskimos.* New York Graphic Society. Boston, MA, 1977.

Collins, George L. *The Art and Politics of Park Planning and Preservation, 1920-1979.* The Bancroft Library. Regional Oral History Office, University of California. Berkeley, CA, 1980.

Collinson, Sir Richard. *Journal of the HMS Enterprise.* London, UK, 1889.

Congress of the United States—
Alaska National Interest Lands Conservation Act—Public Law 96-487. 94 STAT. 2371. Dec. 2, 1980.
Alaska Native Claims Settlement Act—Public Law 92-203. 85 STAT. 688. December 18, 1971.

Connally, Eugenia Horstman, ed. "Wilderness Parklands of Alaska." Articles by Robert Belous, James W. Greenough, and M. Woodbridge Williams. National Parks & Conservation Association. Washington, DC, 1978.

Cook, James. *A Voyage to the Pacific Ocean.* Vols. I and II. London, UK, 1784.

Cook, John A. *Pursuing the Whale.* Houghton Mifflin & Co. Boston, MA, 1926.

Cooper, David J. *Brooks Range Passage.* The Mountaineers. Seattle, WA, 1982.

Crisler, Lois—
Arctic Wild. Harper & Row. New York, NY, 1958.
"Where Wildness is Complete." The Living Wilderness, Vol. 22, No. 60 (Spring 1957).

Davidson, Arthur—
Alakshak The Great Country. Photographs by Art Wolfe. Sierra Club Books. San Francisco, CA, 1989.
"Oil, Caribou and Culture." Defenders of Wildlife, Vol. 67, No. 1 (January/February 1992).

Davis, Neil. *Alaska Science Nuggets.* The Geophysical Institute, University of Alaska. Fairbanks, AK, 1982.

Douglas, William O. *My Wilderness, The Pacific West.* Doubleday & Company, Inc. Garden City, NY, 1960.

Dumond, Don E. *The Eskimos and Aleuts.* Thames and Hudson. London, UK, 1977.

Franklin, Sir John. *Narrative of a Second Expedition.* London, UK, 1828.

Frazier, Duncan. "Edge of the Arctic." National Parks, Vol. 61, No. 11-12 (November/December 1987).

Glover, James A. *A Wilderness Original: The Life of Bob Marshall.* The Mountaineers. Seattle, WA, 1986.

Gryc, George—
"Brooks Range" in *Landscapes of Alaska.* Edited by Howel Williams. Volume I of Part Four. Geology and Geography of the National Park Service's Recreation Survey of Alaska. University of California Press, 1958.
"Arctic Slope" in *Landscapes of Alaska.* Edited by Howel Williams. Volume I of Part Four. Geology and Geography of the National Park Service's Recreation Survey of Alaska. University of California Press, 1958.

Gubser, Nicholas J. *The Nunamiut Eskimos: Hunters of Caribou.* Yale University Press. New Haven, CT, 1965.

Hall, Edwin. In the National Interest: A Geographically Based Study of Anaktuvuk Pass Inupiat Subsistence Through Time. North Slope Borough. Barrow, AK, 1985.

Hanrahan, John and Gruenstein, Peter. *Lost Frontier: The Marketing of Alaska.* W. W. Norton & Company. New York, NY, 1977.

Hanson, Robert A. An Outdoor Challenge Program as a Means of Enhancing Mental Health. Typescript. Community Mental Health Center. Alger and Marquette Counties, MI, 1975.

Hartzog, George B., Jr. *Battling for the National Parks.* Moyer Bell Limited. Mount Kisco, NY, 1988.

Heller, Christine. *Wild Flowers of Alaska.* Graphic Arts Center. Portland, OR, 1966.

Helmericks, Constance and Harmon—
We Live in the Arctic. Little, Brown and Company. Boston, MA, 1947.
The Flight of the Arctic Tern. Little, Brown and Company. Boston, MA, 1952.

Ingstad, Helge. *Nunamiut.* W. W. Norton & Company. New York, NY, 1954.

Jackson, Donald Dale. "The Floor of Creation." Wilderness, Vol. 50, No. 174 (Fall 1986).

Jarvis, D. H., First Lieutenant. "Report of the Cruise of the U.S. Revenue Cutter *Bear,* and the Overland Expedition for the Relief of the Whalers in the Arctic Ocean, From Nov. 27, 1897, to Sept. 13, 1898." United States Revenue Cutter Service. United States Government Printing Office Document #2101. Washington Government Printing Office. Washington, DC, 1899.

Joint Federal–State Land Use Planning Commission for Alaska. The Final Report: Some Guidelines for Deciding Alaska's Future. Anchorage, AK, 1979.

Kauffmann, John M.—
"Noatak." Explorers Journal, Vol. 52, No. 2 (August 1974).

"Noatak." The Living Wilderness, Vol. 38, No. 128 (Winter 1974-75).

"Our Wild and Scenic Rivers—The Noatak." National Geographic Magazine, Vol. 182, No. 1 (July 1977).

Kizzia, Tom—
"Confrontation in the North." Defenders of Wildlife, Vol. 62, No. 5 (September/October 1987).
"Culture at the Crossroads." Defenders of Wildlife, Vol. 62, No. 5 (September/October 1987).

Leffingwell, Ernest de K. The Canning River Region, Northern Alaska. U.S. Geological Survey Professional Paper 109. Washington, DC, 1919.

Leopold, Aldo. A Sand County Almanac. Oxford University Press. New York, NY, 1949.

Leopold, A. Starker and Darling, F. Fraser. Wildlife in Alaska. The New York Zoological Society and The Conservation Foundation. The Ronald Press Company. New York, NY, 1953.

Lopez, Barry—
"In a Country of Light, Among Animals." Outside Magazine, Vol. VI, No. 3 (June/July 1981).
Arctic Dreams. Charles Scribner's Sons. New York, NY, 1986.
Crossig Open Ground. Random House. New York, NY, 1989.

Marshall, Robert—
Alaska Wilderness: Exploring the Central Brooks Range. 2d ed. Edited by George Marshall. The Regents of the University of California. University of California Press. Berkeley, CA, 1970. (First published in 1956 as Arctic Wilderness.)
Arctic Village. The Literary Guild. New York, NY, 1933.

Martin, Calvin—
Keepers of the Game: Indian-Animal Relationships and the Fur Trade. University of California Press. Berkeley, CA, 1978.
"Subarctic Indians and Wildlife." In American Indian Environments. Syracuse University Press, NY, 1980.

McElwaine, Eugene. The Truth about Alaska: The Golden Land of the Midnight Sun. Published by the author. Printed by Regan Printing House, Chicago, IL, 1901.

McGinniss, Joe. Going to Extremes. Alfred A. Knopf. New York, NY, 1980.

McLenegan, S. B. "Exploration of the Noatak River, Alaska." In Report of the Cruise of the Revenue Marine Steamer Corwin in the Arctic Ocean in the Year 1885. By Captain M. A. Healy, U.S.R.M., Commander. Government Printing Office. Washington, DC, 1887.

McPhail, J. D. and Lindsey, C. C. Freshwater Fishes of Northwestern Canada and Alaska. Fisheries Research Board of Canada, Bulletin No. 173. Ottawa, 1970.

McPhee, John—
Coming into the Country. Farrar, Straus and Giroux. New York, NY, 1977. Reprinted from The New Yorker Magazine, 1977.
"The Encircled River." Reprinted from Coming into the Country with added illustrations. The Living Wilderness, Vol. 41, No. 138 and No. 139 (July/September 1977 and October/December 1977).

Meeker, Joseph W. "The People Who Read the Day: Subsistence and Durability." Wilderness, Vol. 50, No. 174 (Fall 1986).

Melham, Tom. 1981. In Alaska's Magnificent Parklands. National Geographic Society. Washington, DC.

Mendenhall, Walter C. "Reconnaissance from Fort Hamlin to Kotzebue Sound by Way of Dall, Kanuti, Allen, and Kowak Rivers." United States Geological Survey Professional Paper No. 10. Washington, DC, 1902.

Mertie, Evelyn. Thirty Summers and a Winter. School of Mineral Industry, University of Alaska.

Mineral Industry Research Laboratory. Fairbanks, AK, 1982.

Miller, Debbie S. *Midnight Wilderness: Journeys in Alaska's National Wildlife Refuge.* Sierra Club Books. San Francisco, CA, 1990.

Mills, Wilbur. "The Central Brooks Range." Alaska Conservation Review (Winter 1974).

Milton, John P. *Nameless Valleys, Shining Mountains.* Walker and Company. New York, NY, 1969.

Mitchell, John G. "In Wildness Was the Preservation of a Smile: An Evocation of Robert Marshall." Wilderness, Vol. 48, No. 169 (Summer 1985).

Mull, C. G., and Adams, K. E., eds. *Dalton Highway, Yukon River to Prudhoe Bay, Alaska: Bedrock Geology of the Eastern Koyukuk Basin, Central Brooks Range, and Eastcentral Arctic Slope.* In Vols. 1 and 2 of *Guidebook 7.* State of Alaska Department of Natural Resources, Division of Geological and Geophysical Surveys. Fairbanks, AK, 1989.

Murie, Margaret E.—
Two in the Far North. Alfred A. Knopf. New York, NY, 1963.
"A Live River in the Arctic." The Living Wilderness, No. 61 (Summer/Fall 1957).
"Return to the Sheenjek." The Living Wilderness, Volume 41, Number 138 (July/September 1977).
"Summer on the Sheenjek." Defenders of Wildlife, Vol. 62, No. 5 (September/October 1987).

Murie, Olaus J.—
"Alaska-Yukon Caribou." North American Fauna No. 54. U.S. Department of Agriculture Bureau of Biological Survey. Washington, DC, 1935.
Journeys to the Far North. The Wilderness Society and American West Publishing Company. Palo Alto, CA, 1973.

Nash, Roderick—
Wilderness and the American Mind. 3d ed. Yale University Press. New Haven, CT, 1982.
"Tourism, Parks and the Wilderness Idea in the History of Alaska." Alaska in Perspective, Vol. IV, No. 1. Alaska Historical Commission and the Alaska Historical Society. Anchorage, AK, 1981.
Comments on the Draft Statement for Management for Gates of the Arctic National Park and Preserve with Emphasis on the Problem of Air Access and Wilderness Values. Santa Barbara, CA, Sept. 10, 1982.

Nelson, Richard K.—
Makes Prayers to the Raven: A Koyukon View of the Northern Forest. The University of Chicago Press. Chicago, IL, 1983.
With Mautner, Kathleen H. and Bane, G. Ray. *Tracks in the Wildland: A Portrayal of Koyukon Nunamiut Subsistence.* Anthropology and Historic Preservation Cooperative Park Studies Unit. University of Alaska. Fairbanks, AK, 1982.

Norton, Boyd. *Alaska Wilderness Frontier.* Reader's Digest Press. New York, NY, 1977.

Orth, Donald J. *Dictionary of Alaska Place Names.* Geological Survey Professional Paper No. 567. United States Government Printing Office. Washington, DC, 1967.

Oswalt, Wendell H. *Eskimos and Explorers.* Chandler & Sharp Publishers, Inc. Novato, CA, 1979.

Parfit, Michael. "Alaska: The Eleventh Hour for America's Wilderness." New Times, Vol. 11, No. 6 (September 1978).

Parker, Walter B. "Future Prospects for Arctic Wildlands in North America." Polar Record (Great Britain), Vol. 20, No. 128 (1981).

Pettyjohn. "The Saga of Lt. Allen." The Alaskana, Vol. 3, No. 2 (April/May 1973).

Rice, Larry. *Gathering Paradise.* Alaska Wilderness Journeys, Fulcrum Publishing. Golden, CO, 1990.

Ricks, Melvin B. *Melvin Ricks' Alaska Bibliography: An Introductory Guide to Alaskan Historical Literature.* Edited by Stephen W. and Betty J. Haycox. Binford and Mort for the Alaska Historical Commission. Portland, OR, 1977.

Ritchie, Robert J. and Childers, Robert A. Preliminary Report: Recreation, Aesthetics and Use of the Arctic National Wildlife Range and Adjacent Areas, Northeastern Alaska. Arctic Gas Biological Report Series, November 1976.

Russell, Andy. *Grizzly Country.* Alfred A. Knopf. New York, NY, 1974.

Schrader, F.C.—

Preliminary Report on a Reconnaissance Along the Chandalar and Koyukuk Rivers, Alaska, in 1899. United States Geological Survey: 21st S.R., Section 1.

"A Reconnaissance in Northern Alaska Across the Rocky Mountains, Along Koyukuk, John, Anaktuvuk, and Colville Rivers, and the Arctic Coast to Cape Lisburne, in 1901." U.S. Geological Survey Professional Paper Number 20. Washington, DC, 1904.

Selkregg, Lidia L. Alaska Regional Profiles: Arctic Region, Vol. II; Northwest Region, Vol. V; Yukon Region, Vol. VI. Arctic Environmental Information and Data Center. University of Alaska. For The State of Alaska Office of the Governor (Jay S. Hammond), and The Joint Federal-State Land Use Planning Commission for Alaska, 1974 et seq.

Sherwood, Morgan B. *Exploration of Alaska 1865-1900.* Yale University Press. New Haven, CT, 1965.

Smith, Philip S.—

The Noatak-Kobuk Region, Alaska. Department of the Interior, United States Geological Survey Bulletin 536. Government Printing Office. Washington, DC, 1913.

"The Alatna-Noatak Region." In *Mineral Resources of Alaska: Report on Progress of Investigations in 1911. See* Brooks, Alfred H. and Others.

With Mertie, J.B., Jr. *Geology and Mineral Resources of Northwestern Alaska.* Department of the Interior, United States Geological Survey Bulletin 815. Government Printing Office. Washington, DC, 1930.

Snyder, Gary. *The Practice of the Wild.* North Point Press. San Francisco, CA, 1990.

Spearman, Grant. "Land Use Values Through Time in the Anaktuvuk Pass Area, North Slope Borough." Anthropology and Historic Preservation Cooperative Park Studies Unit, Occasional Paper No. 22, n.d. University of Alaska. Fairbanks, AK.

Spencer, David L., with Naske, Claus-M., and Carnahan, John. National Wildlife Refuges in Alaska: A Historical Perspective. Arctic Environmental Information and Data Center. Anchorage, AK, January 1979.

Staender, Vivian and Gil. *Our Arctic Year.* Alaska Northwest Publishing Company. Anchorage, AK, 1984.

Standart, Joseph G., III. "North of Doonerak." Wilderness Camping, Vol. 6, No. 5 (February/March 1977).

Stoney, George M., Lieutenant, U.S. Navy. *Explorations in Alaska.* First published in the U.S. Naval Institute Proceedings of September and December 1899. Facsimile 3d ed., The Shorey Book Store. Seattle, WA, 1974.

Stuck, Hudson—

Ten Thousand Miles with a Dog Sled: A Narrative of Winter Travel in Interior Alaska. Charles Scribner's Sons. New York, NY, 1928.

A Winter Circuit of Our Arctic Coast. Charles Scribner's Sons. New York, NY, 1920.

Sumner, Lowell and Collins, George L. "Arctic Wilderness." The Living Wilderness, Number 47 (Winter 1953-54).

Thayer, A. S. "The Arctic National Wildlife Range." Alaska Sportsman. September 1967.

United States Department of State. Draft Environmental Impact Statement for the Agreement Between the United States and Canada for the Conservation of Migratory Caribou. March, 1980.

United States Department of the Interior, Alaska Planning Group—
Proposed Gates of the Arctic National Wilderness Park and Nunamiut National Wildlands. Draft Environmental Impact Statement. Washington, DC, 1973.
Final Environmental Impact Statements, Washington, DC: Proposed Arctic National Wildlife Refuge, 1974. Proposed Gates of the Arctic National Park, 1974. Proposed Kobuk Valley National Monument, 1975. Proposed Noatak National Arctic Range, 1974. Proposed Cape Krusenstern National Monument, 1974. Proposed Alaska Maritime National Wildlife Refuge, 1974.

United States Department of the Interior, Fish and Wildlife Service. Arctic National Wildlife Refuge: Summary of the Final Comprehensive Conservation Plan, Environmental Impact Statement, Wilderness Review, and Wild River Plans. Anchorage, AK, 1988.

United States Department of the Interior, National Park Service—
Final Environmental Impact Statement. Wilderness Recommendation: Gates of the Arctic National Park and Preserve. Anchorage, AK, 1986.
General Management Plan. Enviromental Assessment, Land Protection Plan: Cape Krusen Stern National Monument. Anchorage, AK, 1986.
General Management Plan. Environmental Assessment, Land Protection Plan: Kobuk Valley National Park. Anchorage, AK, 1986.
General Management Plan. Environmental Assessment, Wilderness Suitability Review: Gates of the Arctic National Park. Anchorage AK, 1986.
General Management Plan. Land Protection Plan, Wilderness Suitability Review: Noatak National Preserve. Anchorage, AK, 1986.

University of British Columbia Law Review. "Proceedings of the Arctic International Wildlife Range Conference: October 21 and 22, 1970." Vol. 6, No. 1, Supplement. Vancouver, British Columbia, Canada, June 1971.

Viereck, L.A. and Little, E.L. *Alaska Trees and Shrubs*. U.S. Dept. of Agriculture. Forest Service. Agricultural Handbook No. 410, 1972.

Watkins, T.H.—
Vanishing Arctic: Alaska's National Wildlife Refuge. Aperture Foundation, Inc., New York, NY; in association with The Wilderness Society, Washington, DC, 1988.
"A Measure of Fragility." Wilderness, Vol. 50, No. 174 (Fall 1986).
"The Perils of Expedience, Ten Years After Passage of the Alaska Lands Act . . ." Wilderness, Vol. 54, No. 191 (Winter 1990).

Watt, Richard Darrell. "The Recreational Potential of the Arctic National Wildlife Refuge." Master of Science Thesis, University of Alaska. Fairbanks, AK, 1966.

Weeden, Robert B. *Alaska: Promises to Keep*. Houghton Mifflin Company. Boston, MA, 1978.

Williss, G. Frank. "Do Things Right the First Time": The National Park Service and the Alaska National Interest Lands Conservation Act of 1980. U.S. Department of the Interior/National Park Service. U.S. Government Printing Office. Denver Service Center, NPS D-81, September 1985.

Wright, Billie. *Four Seasons North*. Harper & Row. New York, NY, 1973.

Wright, Sam. *Koviashuvik: A Time and Place of Joy*. Sierra Club Books. San Francisco, CA, 1988.

Wuerthner, George. *Alaska's Mountain Ranges*. American Geographic Publishing. Helena, MT, 1988.

Yale School of Forestry and Environmental Studies. Proceedings of Alaska Lands Symposium. New Haven, CT, April 1979.

Young, Steven B.—

To the Arctic: An Introduction to the Far Northern World. John Wiley & Sons, Inc. New York, NY, 1989.

Editor. The Environment of the Noatak River Basin, Alaska. The Center for Northern Studies. Wolcott, VT, 1974.

Zwinger, Ann H. and Willard, Beatrice E., Ph.D. *Land Above the Tree: A Guide to American Alpine Tundra.* Harper & Row. New York, NY, 1972.

INDEX

John M. Kauffmann's twenty years with the
National Park Service included six as chief
planner for Alaska's Gates of the Arctic National Park and Preserve and Noatak National
Preserve in Alaska's Brooks Range. He has
engaged in and headed numerous field studies
and planning efforts in the East and Pacific
Northwest. A former journalist, he wrote and
edited for the Department of Interior, and is
the author of Flow East: A Look at Our North
Atlantic Rivers. Kauffmann has served on the
governing boards of The Wilderness Society,
American Rivers, the National Parks and Conservation Association, and the Natural Resources Council of Maine, among others. He
now resides in Mount Desert, Maine.

The author above Hammond River. National
Park Service photograph by Bill Resor)

The MOUNTAINEERS, founded in 1906, is a non-profit outdoor activity and conservation club, whose mission is "to explore, study, preserve and enjoy the natural beauty of the outdoors. . . ." Based in Seattle, Washington, the club is now the third largest such organization in the United States, with 12,000 members and four branches throughout Washington State.

The Mountaineers sponsors both classes and year-round outdoor activities in the Pacific Northwest, which include hiking, mountain climbing, ski-touring, snowshoeing, bicycling, camping, kayaking and canoeing, nature study, sailing, and adventure travel. The club's conservation division supports environmental causes through educational activities, sponsoring legislation, and presenting informational programs. All club activities are led by skilled, experienced volunteers, who are dedicated to promoting safe and responsible enjoyment and preservation of the outdoors.

The Mountaineers Books, an active, non-profit publishing program of the club, produces guidebooks, instructional texts, historical works, natural history guides, and works on environmental conservation. All books produced by The Mountaineers are aimed at fulfilling the club's mission.

If you would like to participate in these organized outdoor activities or the club's programs, consider a membership in The Mountaineers. For information and an application, write or call The Mountaineers, Club Headquarters, 300 Third Avenue West, Seattle, Washington 98119; (206) 284-6310.

Send or call for our catalog of over 200 outdoor books:
The Mountaineers Books
1011 SW Klickitat Way, Suite 107
Seattle, WA 98134
1-800-553-4453

~

(Continue from page 2) * Excerpts from *Alaska Wilderness: Exploring the Central Brooks Range, Second Edition*, by Robert Marshall, edited by George Marshall, are reprinted with permission of the University of California Press. Copyright (c) 1970 by The Regents of the University of California. * Excerpts from *Nunamiut*, by Helge Ingstad, are reprinted by permission of W.W. Norton & Company. Copyright (c) 1954 by Helge Ingstad. * Excerpts from *Arctic Wild*, by Lois Crisler, are reprinted with permission of HarperCollins Publishers. Copyright (c) 1958 by Lois Crisler. * Excerpts from "The People Who Read the Day," (*Wilderness* magazine, Fall 1986), by Joseph W. Meeker; "Where the Wilderness is Complete," by Lois Crisler (*The Living Wilderness* magazine [now *Wilderness* magazine], Spring 1957) are reprinted with permission of T. H. Watkins. * Excerpts from *Vanishing Arctic: Alaska's National Wildlife Refuge*, by T. H. Watkins, published by Aperture in association with The Wilderness Society, are reprinted by permission of T. H. Watkins. Copyright (c) 1988 by the Aperture Foundation. * Excerpts from *Nameless Valleys, Shining Mountains*, by John Milton, are reprinted by permission from Walker and Company. Copyright (c) 1970 by John Milton. * Excerpts from *The Practice of the Wild*, by Gary Snyder, are reprinted with permission of Farrar, Straus & Giroux, Inc. * Excerpts from *We Live in the Arctic* and *The Flight of the Arctic Tern*, by Constance and Harmon Helmericks, are reprinted courtesy of Harmon Helmericks. * The poem "The Brooks Range" first appeared in the Spring 1991 issue of "Voices," a literary magazine for College of the Atlantic, Bar Harbor, Maine.